This book is dedicated to my four beautiful children
Jacy Charlie Nicholls, Ambrose Wakem Geoffrey Nicholls, Harry Elliot Nicholls and Ellie Charlotte Nicholls

It is also dedicated to two great mentors and friends,
Chris Hamilton and Bernard Whimpress

Wakefield Press

Playing to Win

Barry Nicholls is a former A-grade district cricketer who has written about sports for 30 years. He broadcast various daily programs on ABC Radio for nearly two decades and lives in Perth, Western Australia. This is his tenth book.

By the same author

Triple Blue: Jack Oatey, John Wynne and the Whole Damned Thing

The Story of '78: How Norwood Gave Sturt the Blues

Cricket Dreaming: The Rites of Summer

For Those Who Wait: The Barry Jarman Story

You Only Get One Innings: Family, Mates and the Wisdom of Cricket

The Test of the Century: The Story Behind 1977's Centenary Test

The Pocket History of the Ashes: All you need to know about cricket's greatest contest

Second Innings: On Men, Mental Health and Cricket

The Establishment Boys: The Other Side of Kerry Packer's Cricket Revolution

Playing to Win

Ian Chappell's 1972 Australians

Barry Nicholls

Wakefield
Press

Wakefield Press
16 Rose Street
Mile End
South Australia 5031
www.wakefieldpress.com.au

First published 2025

Edited by Julia Beaven, Wakefield Press
Typeset by Jesse Pollard, Wakefield Press

ISBN 978 1 92304 284 1

NATIONAL LIBRARY OF AUSTRALIA

A catalogue record for this book is available from the National Library of Australia

CORIOLE McLAREN VALE

Wakefield Press thanks Coriole Vineyards for continued support

Supported by a grant from the Government of South Australia

Contents

Foreword by Ian Chappell

When I read a summary of the 1972 tour of the UK more than 50 years after the event the thing that stood out was the players' enjoyment.

Despite the grinding nature and ridiculous programming, overall the 1972 tour was an enjoyable one. It also provided the Australian team with a watershed moment, as following the victory in the Fifth Test at The Oval I felt we could beat any team we faced.

In looking back on the tour there are a couple of strong memories. First, was the pleasing manner in which a number of those players achieved distinction in their life after cricket. That success spoke of the players' intelligence and their desire to succeed.

Unfortunately the passing of time has also resulted in the loss of some good people and some very close mates. In chronological order the passing of Johnny Gleeson, Graeme Watson, Ashley Mallett, Rod Marsh, Brian Taber and Keith Stackpole has been very hard to take; they were all good people whose company I enjoyed.

Luckily I've stayed in touch with many of the players from 1972. In my commentary days I looked forward to the occasions when in Melbourne Keith Stackpole [the excellent vice-captain] and in Perth Dennis Lillee arranged dinner with a number of ex-players.

The Australian team developed into a tight-knit unit. It's a little known fact that two of the players who were unceremoniously dumped from the 1972 tour contributed to that success.

In the game against Leicestershire in 1972, I stood on the balcony after play one night while Graham McKenzie happily discussed the strengths and weaknesses of potential England players.

In 1973/74 when Ian Redpath was belatedly returned to the Australian side that toured New Zealand I asked him if he'd consider opening to help out the team. I told Redda he'd be in the team whether he opened or not and typical of his unselfishness, he immediately replied, 'I'd be happy to open.'

Another thing that stood out for me in reading the book was some of the codswallop that was written about the touring team.

The accusations of excessive swearing on the field were particularly galling and aside from being incorrect they were most unfair on the Australian players. The article that Ted Dexter wrote about the Australians use of lip salve to shine the ball was not only wrong but it also contained a glaring mistake.

Dexter expounded a theory that 'lip ice' was the culprit. One big problem with that ridiculous theory is the Australians don't use 'lip ice', that was a South African trait.

The accusation was a giant slur on Bob Massie's amazing debut Test achievement in taking 16 wickets at Lord's but unfortunately my email on the subject to Dexter was left unanswered when Ted died suddenly in 2021. Massie was quite rightly extremely annoyed at Dexter's incorrect accusation.

The Australian team became a very confident, aggressive bunch but it was ignorant and entirely wrong to label us arrogant. If a team doesn't have confidence in its ability then it can be very difficult to win.

My upbringing taught me it was best to try and win the game from ball one and that is the way the team played. I have only ever found one reason to play cricket and that is to try to win. Cricket is not a statistical exercise.

With that in mind it was extremely satisfying for Greg and I to become the first brothers to score a century on the same day and innings of a Test match. We both felt that we were partly repaying our parents Martin and Jeanne for everything they had sacrificed to give us the opportunity to represent Australia.

It was extra satisfying that brother Trevor was at The Oval with Martin and Jeanne to witness our success that day.

On the 1972 tour we were fortunate to have the services of four very passionate officials. However it was manager Ray Steele's foreword in my book *Tigers among the Lions* that gave me great personal satisfaction.

In the book Steele, a veteran administrator, wrote: 'This was the least average-conscious side with which I have toured and credit must go to Ian for that.'

The Australian team was also fortunate to have a large and vibrant media contingent on tour that mixed well with the squad. This was highlighted by journalist Mike Coward's excellent singing at the Pontarddulais Rugby Club, which helped save face for the Australian team. Despite often enjoying the company of team members they maintained their journalistic integrity.

It is satisfying for the players that the 1972 Australian tour has been recognised for its contribution to the game of cricket. The players can be extremely proud of their efforts and even more so for the many who suffered financial hardship because of the minuscule payment on the long and demanding tour.

I'm delighted Barry Nicholls has seen fit to recognise the importance of the tour with this comprehensive book. I thank him on behalf of the players and wish him all the best in his endeavours.

Ian Chappell, 2025

Foreword by Dennis Lillee

Reading the book *Playing to Win* cover to cover brought back so many great memories of the 1972 tour.

This was my first tour with an official Australian team, along with many other players on their first tour. It was an exciting time heading to the unknown, with the result being the start of a long era of success for our Test side. The nucleus of the team became the mainstay of a dominant side for more than a decade.

The conduit for this success was our great captain, Ian Chappell. He is a superb bloke, a great player and the best captain I played under for Australia. Ian melded a group of young individuals into a tough, hard-nosed team who knew how to win.

It was also a time of realisation that we, as players, could not continue to spend six months away touring, book-ended with home season Sheffield Shield games and Test matches. Something had to give. We were semi-professional but had to hold down jobs as well to make ends meet. There were no contracts between the Australian Cricket Board and players then so it was a game-by-game proposition, with no certainty of income. Our employers could only give us so much time off, and payment for a six-month tour of the United Kingdom was £1200, with $200 per Test match at home (i.e. $1000 for a five Test series and $40 for a Shield game). This caused problems going forward.

Boiling point was around the corner and despite attempts by Ian

Chappell to negotiate with the Australian Cricket Board to improve our lot, it fell on deaf ears! We, a team of winning but disgruntled blokes, were becoming more and more militant and were very close to engaging in strike action in order to push our cause.

Fortunately that did not eventuate as Kerry Packer emerged in the nick of time to change cricket, and the cricketers' lot forever.

What you see with cricket today is a direct result of Ian and his loyal team-mates becoming a hugely successful team, a team that would help change the face of our great game. In my opinion, this is why the 1972 tour of the UK was so important in the history of cricket.

Dennis Lillee, 2025

Introduction

Australia's 1972 cricket tour of England was more than a sporting event; it was a reflection of societal change. The once conservative, defensive and angular Bill Lawry was replaced by a new era of leadership, embodied by the salty-mouthed, squinting, and 'ready to take you on' Ian Chappell. The Australians, under Chappell, played to win, a significant shift in the team's approach. The make-up of the team changed, with the emergence of the dominant, alpha-male personalities of Ian and Greg Chappell, Dennis Lillee and Rod Marsh, men who now questioned every action taken by cricket administrators. Chappell's new leadership style transformed the game, reflecting and influencing the broader societal context.

Britain had been at the heart of the Swinging Sixties but, by 1972, the shine had worn off. Tradition prevailed among social, industrial and political upheaval. Nearly two decades after Queen Elizabeth's coronation, royalty remained as popular as ever. Marriage rates peaked while British car production and local manufacturing steadily declined. Despite most houses being equipped with colour televisions, fridges and washing machines, living standards were starting to plateau. Relatively low unemployment had surpassed one million for the first time since 1930, doubling in just two years. England remained fiercely masculine despite the nascent progress in women's rights. Tension simmered between the white working class and immigrants from the Indian subcontinent and the Caribbean, reflected in popular – unquestioned – TV shows such as *Love Thy Neighbour*. Union membership was expected; the mining unions powerful. For seven weeks from February, mining strikes led Prime Minister Edward Heath to declare a State of Emergency (one of five called in just over three years) as the country experienced a series of power outages lasting up to nine hours. The Troubles in Northern Ireland escalated throughout the year, leading the British government to introduce Direct Rule over Northern Ireland. The sense of optimism from the 1960s had dissolved.

The previous summer, the national cricket side had shown signs of decline – with India winning a series for the first time in England. Despite this, the conservative order of the Marylebone Cricket Club persisted. Selectors prioritised caution over adventure and youth, retaining 40-year-old Ray Illingworth as captain. There were many questions to be answered, including whether the home side could hold on to the Ashes they had fought so hard to win back on that long, arduous campaign down under in 1970/71.

When Ian Chappell's Australians arrived in London in mid-April, they entered a unique social and cultural landscape. The English fans, known for their genuine love of the game, warmly welcomed the broad-shouldered, tanned and muscular-looking team. Their captain, dressed in a safari suit, boldly announced their intention to play attacking cricket. Despite the press labelling Chappell's side as the worst to tour England, their spirit and determination remained unshaken, serving as a powerful motivation for all who witnessed their resilience.

Fifty years ago, Ashes tours lasted six months and were packed with 26 first-class matches, five Tests, several so-called friendly fixtures, and three one-day internationals. The series attracted enormous public interest, with 370,000 spectators paying a world record of half-a-million pounds to attend the Tests. On the other side of the world, more than 15 million phone calls were made to the Post Office Scores service in Australia to check progress.

The summer confirmed the reputations of Dennis Lillee, Greg Chappell and Rod Marsh, who all played pivotal roles. Ian Chappell's attacking captaincy was vindicated and admired worldwide. Cricket was almost back to the force it had been after the Second World War. However, with growing player frustration surrounding pay and conditions, the seed for future revolution had also been sown. This book follows the footsteps of the touring Australians in that English summer of 1972, and their profound impact on the game.

Prologue

Ian Chappell was perched on a stool at the bar of the Overway Hotel in Hindley Street as the lunchtime crowd bustled past on their way to the thoroughfare leading to the Adelaide Railway Station. The critics were off Chappell's back after he had scored his second century of the 1970/71 Ashes summer in the Sixth Test. The press had long aimed at Australia's top order for failing to combat England's firebrand opening bowlers John Snow and Bob Willis and, before that, the South African pace duo of Peter Pollock and Mike Procter.

That day, Chappell was enjoying a schnitzel pub lunch and two schooners between jobs as a sales rep for cigarette company W.D. & H.O. Wills when the barman approached. 'There's a phone call for you.'

Chappell picked up the receiver and heard the voice of former SA teammate Alan 'Sheffield' Shiell.

'Congratulations. You're the captain of Australia.'

'Bullshit, you're joking,' Chappell replied.

'They've sacked Lawry. You're the captain.'

Chappell couldn't believe it. He leaned back in his chair and ordered another beer.

'Shit, captain of Australia.'

Lawry, meanwhile, found out he'd been dropped while listening to the radio. When Chappell arrived home, he greeted his wife Kay with the news and, referring to the manner of Lawry's dumping, the line that would define his time as captain of the Australian cricket team: 'The bastards will never get me like that.'

That afternoon, the Adelaide *Advertiser* team was at Chappell's home, snapping the new skipper with his young daughter, Amanda. The next day's front-page lede was written; Ian Chappell was now the 34th captain of Australia. As the news sunk in, Chappell reflected on Lawry's dumping as captain. It seemed a fair decision, though he still considered Lawry a Test-class batsman. It was the way the selectors handled the matter, without even telling Lawry (he'd sat for most of the previous day's play with selector Sam Loxton) that rankled with Chappell.

Ian Chappell had a few things to consider. One was the side's lack of experience. His front-line bowlers – Dennis Lillee, Terry Jenner and Kerry O'Keeffe – had played one Test. Left-arm paceman Tony Dell and opening batsman Ken Eastwood were about to debut, Greg Chappell and Rodney Marsh had just started their Test careers. He also took stock of the captains he had played under. He wanted to be aggressive like Les Favell but avoid his habit of yelling at teammates if things went wrong. He might set a defensive field like Bill Lawry to suffocate a batsman, but take more risks to win. Ian Chappell resembled his grandfather, former Test captain and South Australian sporting great Vic Richardson, in many ways. 'If you can't be a good cricketer, at least look like one,' was his maternal grandfather's advice.

Chappell always looked immaculate in cricket whites – spick and span – and displayed a batting technique honed at 4 Leak Avenue, Gray-more, an Adelaide suburb home to many young families after the Sec-ond World War. Ian's father Martin, a state baseballer who was a good enough batsman to lead the A grade district aggregate in 1950/51, was a stern taskmaster. He started his young sons playing with a cricket ball in the 24-metre-wide backyard, allowing for a full-length turf pitch made from clay soil used on the Adelaide Oval wickets. The house was on the off side, with glass louvres on the back porch, so many windows were broken until Martin installed wire mesh gates to protect the glass. It was Lynn Fuller, as coach, who offered an eight-year-old Ian Chappell the best advice: 'Son, it doesn't matter how good a coach I am, I can't help you in the middle, so the quicker you learn the game for yourself the better off you'll be.'

At 13, Ian Chappell was playing senior cricket at Prince Alfred College, the alma mater of Australian greats Joe Darling and Clem Hill. In 1963/64, aged 19, a blazing 149 for South Australia against a New South Wales attack featuring Alan Davidson, Richie Benaud and Johnny Martin had the scribes singing Chappell's praises. Australian honours arrived against the visiting Pakistan side in 1964. While missing the West Indies tour in 1965, he was restored to the national side at the end of the 1965/66 Ashes series (before playing 36 consecutive Test matches across four continents leading into the 1972 Ashes tour). He was promoted to bat at number three by Lawry for the home series against the West Indies in 1968/69. Sir Donald Bradman had told him, 'You can make the game from there.' He would in more ways than one.

Chapter One

The background

In October 1970, just three weeks after Carlton's famous come-from-behind Victorian Football League (VFL) grand final win against Collingwood in front of 121,696 at the MCG, the Marylebone Cricket Club (MCC) tourists arrived in Adelaide for a long, hot, drawn-out summer of cricket.

The Test series began with two high-scoring drawn matches in Brisbane and Perth. Greg Chappell's hundred on debut at the first-ever WACA Test Match was followed by the Melbourne washout, enabling the inaugural one-day international, attracting a crowd of 46,006. The Fourth Test at Sydney featured Geoff Boycott's second innings of 142 off 360 balls and the 'Snow invasion'. John Snow's seven second-inning wickets filleted the top order of the Australian side and they collapsed to be all out for 116. Bill Lawry carried his bat for the second time in just over a year, and England won by 299 runs. In the rescheduled Melbourne Test, England barely moved into second gear, not bothering to chase the target of 269 in four hours. The Adelaide Test witnessed the arrival of Dennis Lillee. His five-wicket haul on debut and Boycott's refusal to go when run out both thrilled and amused Australian cricket fans. The summer of caution continued when England declined to enforce the follow-on. Keith Stackpole and Ian Chappell batted together for over six hours, adding 198 to the drawn game. Australia lost the final encounter at the SCG by 62 runs and, with it, the series and the Ashes in a controversial match where

Illingworth, in protest of crowd behaviour, led his side briefly from the field.

On 25 February 1971, John Snow's flight jetted out of Darwin in muggy, overcast skies, heading to London. As the plane banked and made its way across the Arafura Sea, England's key pace bowler reflected on the past five months touring Australia. The tourists' win in the Seventh Test, and its champagne and beer-laden hangover, sat heavily on Snow's mind. Leaning back in his seat, he felt a tingle in his little finger from injuring his hand on the picket fence while attempting a catch. As he placed his left palm on his smashed right hand, Snow contemplated a more determined stance against dictatorial and incompetent cricket administrators. Snow had witnessed the enormous chasm between players and officialdom for years. He thought England skipper Ray Illingworth had handled his players well, even if the team management didn't. Illingworth's ability to lead the prickly England quick was the key to success. 'You'll never bowl more than 20 overs in one day for me in conditions like this,' Illingworth told Snow, aware of his ability to get tremendous lift off a length and move the ball off the seam on the hard Australian pitches. Under Illingworth, the MCC had become the first touring side to reclaim the Ashes since Douglas Jardine's Bradman-blunting Bodyline side of 1932/33.

Despite England's success, concerns about administrator incompetence grew. Illingworth believed team manager David Clark focused more on empire building than winning. When Clark criticised the approach of both Test captains to the Australian press (claiming 'too many bouncers'), the comments understandably jarred. That Illingworth only became aware of Clark's remarks after a 6.30 am call from the press made it more galling. These were different times. Player power had yet to ascend, the officials called the shots. Administrators made decisions on behalf of the players without consultation. When the Third Test at Melbourne was washed out, a Seventh Test at Sydney was scheduled. The England players found out when Sir Donald Bradman said, 'It's very nice of you fellows to agree to play the extra game.' Clark, Bradman and MCC Treasurer Gubby Allen had made the decision. Snow later wrote, 'It was hard enough that we should get the news; even worse, we had not been told by one of our officials.'

The change meant 20 days of Test cricket in the final 40 days of England's stay. Illingworth, by then 38 and having toured Australia almost a decade before, knew the challenge of playing six Tests throughout 40-degree days, eight ball overs, as well as four-day state games and country fixtures. By scheduling a Seventh Test, Australia gained a chance to even the series and earn an extra full match fee while England's touring costs were fixed. Illingworth eventually extracted a £25 fee per player from MCC assistant secretary Donald Carr. It wasn't much, but it was the same as the captain's allowance (introduced to ensure the captain wasn't paid less than some players, whose tour payment was partly based on overseas experience).

It wasn't just the lengthy tour that was providing niggles. If the players wanted their wives to join them, they had to pay their way and accommodation. Manager Clark, however, was accompanied by his wife and sisters, who stayed in what Illingworth considered the 'team room'. Illingworth's room ended up being the area where the players met.

While this played out off-field, the Australian vice-captain Ian Chappell watched on, admiring Ray Illingworth's captaincy. He observed how Illingworth mapped out the 1970/71 series in which 12 of the original 17 in the MCC touring party had never played Test cricket in Australia. Illingworth was canny. In that protracted summer, England won the Ashes, yet victory came in only three of their 14 first-class matches on tour, one against Tasmania, at that stage a non-Sheffield Shield-playing state. Ian Chappell observed, 'I learned a lot by watching how Illingworth handled John Snow, which helped me with Dennis Lillee. Ray had an understanding with Snow, who would always elevate his performance when it mattered the most. Ray kept attacking and let the batsman know you were trying to get him out.'

Illingworth led by example when he took his players from the field during the final Test at Sydney after unruly crowd members threw cans and bottles onto the ground. Even when it looked like England might forfeit the match, Illingworth was unmoved. 'Clark [team manager] was running around like a chook with its head cut off, but I knew the Ashes were not as important as player safety.'

When Ray Illingworth left Australia in February 1971, he knew the next Ashes contest would prove even more challenging. He had noticed Dennis Lillee at the WACA in Perth before the Second Test. 'When Lillee turned Boycott's cap around, I thought, hello, we've got a live one here.' He discovered more when Lillee took five wickets on debut at the Adelaide Test. Illingworth also knew that any team containing the Chappell brothers, Stackpole and Marsh was not to be taken lightly. Alan Knott rated Rod Marsh as a keeper despite his troubled start to Test cricket. Marsh's soft hands and footwork speed behind the stumps were hard to match.

Public interest in the 1970/71 series was huge. The total television audience was estimated to be more than 30 million, with an average of a million viewers watching each day's play on the ABC (Australia's population was 12.7 million in 1971). That summer saw the first national TV coverage that led to an increase in live crowds. Real-time replays were added to the broadcast, including daily highlights featuring Richie Benaud and Frank Tyson. Some 678,486 people attended the seven Test series (one washed out), with a gate of $532,220. The average daily attendance was more than 20,000. Despite the game's popularity, former South Australian and Australian Services player and journalist R.S. 'Dick' Whitington despaired at the state of Ashes cricket. In *Captains Outrageous? Cricket in the Seventies,* Whitington described the 1970/71 series as 'perhaps the least attractive' Test cricket he had seen. Ray Illingworth, Whitington noted, had 'dragged dedication around Australia for 103 days last summer – for longer than it took Napoleon to quit Elba, march on Paris, regain control of France and lose Waterloo'. The respective captains had 'dismissed from Test cricket, all delight, all adventure'. After watching ten overs in the first hour, as Australia batted in Adelaide, South African Barry Richards, the South Australian import, labelled the English bowlers' efforts as 'appalling' and called for a new law to increase over rates. 'Something must be done before spectators throw more than empty beer cans over the pickets.' The critics needn't have worried because a new Australian captain, who would eventually help revolutionise the game, was on the horizon.

Ian Chappell as captain

It's no secret that as the 1970s progressed, Ian Chappell and Sir Donald Bradman had numerous conflicts. But the resentment had barely begun when Chappell was first selected as Australian captain at the end of the 1970/71 summer. Fatefully, one of Bradman's final acts as Chairman of Selectors was to appoint Ian Chappell as Australian captain. Bradman signed off on the appointment, but it was Neil Harvey who convinced Bradman the decision was a sound one.

'It was fucking me,' Harvey said as he pointed at his chest many years later following a round of golf with Ian Chappell, who had just asked how he was given the captaincy. Chappell always had time for Harvey; he was a player he greatly admired and an administrator he respected. The respect was mutual.

While Chappell's elevation surprised some in the Adelaide Establishment, logic was behind the move. He was the Australian vice-captain and fresh from a successful summer with the bat against England, with centuries in the two preceding Tests in 1970/71. He was also on his way to captaining South Australia to a Shield win in that season (with the help of South African Barry Richards). Ian's younger brother Greg had debuted with a ton in the historic Perth Test. The Chappell brothers represented the future of Australian cricket. The 1930s Australian opening batsman and now cricket writer Jack Fingleton (an ally of Chappell's grandfather Vic Richardson) soon became a confidante of the new Australian captain, even though he made it known that he disliked Chappell's swearing. Chappell would wind up the 'old square', while Fingleton saw Chappell as a 'young mod'.

Ian Chappell led by example. He batted at the crucial number-three spot for Australia and was respected by his teammates. When he faced up, he did so with a look of steely determination. He was gritty and capable of holding his own against the most hostile bowling. Chappell was also a wonderful slips fieldsman. When Bill Lawry was dropped for the Seventh Test, Illingworth wasn't disappointed. 'I felt we'd get better cricket, and Ian's approach allowed you to open the game up. He was always very positive and knew when to attack and defend but not in the way that would let your opposition know.'

The dispatched Lawry was ever the pragmatist, while Ian Chappell looked to the leadership flair and style of Richie Benaud. Chappell wore his shirt unbuttoned, just like Benaud had. He also used to look skywards to adjust his eyesight to the sun, just like Benaud when he walked out to bat. Chappell observed Benaud's ability to read the play and work batsmen out and liked the way Benaud took the game up to the opposition, not afraid to make difficult decisions. Benaud could make players feel like they were better than they were. He made his players believe they could win even if the cause looked hopeless.

The style of Australian captaincy had changed, and by 1972 society was also undergoing a significant shift. In December, Labor under Gough Whitlam would be swept into power, ending 23 years of Federal conservative leadership on promises including improving women's rights, free tertiary education, the withdrawal of troops from Vietnam and a significant expansion of the arts community. Change was indeed in the air.

Summer of 1971/72

Cricket fans were expecting a five-Test series against South Africa, a side considered the best in the world, as administrators salivated at the anticipated crowds and gate profits. In September 1971, Sir Donald Bradman, as Chairman of the Australian Board of Control for international cricket – which became the Australian Cricket Board in 1973 and is now Cricket Australia – announced the South African tour was cancelled following the disrupted Springbok rugby side's winter visit in that year. As Mike Coward wrote in *The Chappell Years: Cricket in the '70s,* 'When it came to competing against South Africa, Australian cricket could no longer distance itself from the harsh realities of the cricket world.' When Garry Sobers agreed to lead a Rest of the World side against Australia, a summer of international cricket was confirmed. That it happened owed much to the special connection between Bradman and Sobers that began when the West Indies toured Australia in 1960/61 and continued when the West Indian great played domestic cricket for South Australia for the next three seasons.

Bradman knew the value of the Australians gaining international experience before the 1972 Ashes. Still, the Rest of the World squad, picked by Bradman with advice from Sobers, was more an affable and politically sound mix of players than an actual world eleven. It included three South Africans and was selected with an eye to diplomacy. All the Test-playing nations were included, but the absence of John Snow, Mike Procter, Eddie Barlow and Barry Richards made the side barely representative of what the Rest of the World might offer.

The 17-man Rest of the World squad consisted of Garry Sobers, Zaheer Abbas, Hylton Ackerman, Intikhab Alam, Bishan Bedi, Bob Cunis, Farokh Engineer, Sunil Gavaskar, Norman Gifford, Tony Greig, Richard Hutton, Rohan Kanhai, Clive Lloyd, Asif Masood, Graeme Pollock, Peter Pollock (both because of other commitments were unable to tour until the completion of the first two Tests) and Bob Taylor.

Individual displays of greatness revealed more than studying just the match results. The First Test in Brisbane saw five centuries in one game, including Ian Chappell's brace of hundreds. The second in Perth revealed the fire and brimstone of Dennis Lillee, hair wildly bouncing around almost in synchronicity with his splayed arms, taking 12 wickets on a lightning-quick WACA pitch (staggeringly, nine batsmen were dismissed in the first session on the second day). Lillee's first innings, 8 for 29 from 57 balls, warned batsmen worldwide.

In Melbourne, Sobers' freewheeling second innings of 254 helped the visitors to 514 on an improving pitch. That 38,179 attended the MCG on 3 January to witness the first 139 runs of Sobers' knock confirmed that public interest in the series was high. Two days later (after a rest day), close to 30,000 watched stage two of Sobers' masterpiece. Bradman described it as 'the best innings ever seen in Australia'. The words echoed down the years as Sobers' innings became a template for excellence (Bradman even commissioned and commentated on a film of highlights to be shown to cricket clubs around the country). The 254 runs from 323 balls with 33 boundaries and two sixes provided the best advertisement the series could get. Greg Chappell's undefeated 115 and Doug Walters' 127 (including a 100 before lunch) in Australia's second innings are often forgotten in the aftermath of the Sobers' mauling.

In Sydney, the Chappell brothers became the first siblings to score hundreds in the same innings of an international game. Australia could easily have won the series if fortunes had differed, with torrential rain at the Sydney Test, saving the tourists on the final day. Match crowd aggregates confirmed the success of the tour. Melbourne's attendance was 133,638, Sydney's 90,961 and Adelaide's 61,737. The Rest of the World took the rubber 2–1 with a nine-wicket win on the fourth day in Adelaide. The crowd total for the five 'Test' series 324,497.

Greg Chappell believed the series was crucial to brother Ian's development as a captain – 'the series helped Ian and gave him more captaincy experience, perhaps in a slightly less tense atmosphere than a series against South Africa'. Ian disagrees. 'I was always learning, but I didn't feel different about captaining any game. If we'd been losing all the time, I wouldn't have been captaining an Australian team to England in 1972.' For Australia, the Rest of the World tour had another significance.

One who would come to know the perils of national leadership during tumultuous times was South African-born Tony Greig. Greig, included in the side at the insistence of Sobers, earned his international stripes, taking 16 wickets at 27 and scoring 525 runs at 37.50. At over two metres in height, broad-shouldered and thin-hipped, Greig bounced into bowl at a medium pace and drove the ball on the up with an assurance that matched his gregarious, outspoken nature. Born in Queenstown, South Africa, Greig was not yet qualified to play Test cricket for England. He split his time between living in England, where he played for Sussex, and South Africa, working at St Andrews College, Grahamstown, near Port Elizabeth as a physical education teacher and cricket coach. Former Australian leg spinner Bill O'Reilly thought Greig was the 'best all-rounder we have seen come out of England for some time'. Only time would tell if O'Reilly's assessment was accurate.

The international summer also provided a finishing school for Greg Chappell and Dennis Lillee. Greg learned some of the subtleties of batting while watching Graeme Pollock effortlessly carve out 136 in Adelaide. The younger Chappell admired Pollock's minimalist approach at the crease. 'I was staggered at how little movement (Pollock) made . . . he always got his body in the right position, and his balance was good.' Greg also learned during post-match dressing room beers the value of heavier bats. Pollock's blade was twice as heavy as the one he used. Greg moved in increments, using a two-pound six-ounce bat, to one weighing two pounds eight ounces. He also altered his mental approach to the game, realising his poor early season form in 1971/72 was partly due to fundamental errors in concentration. Greg studied the psychological side of batting closely, concluding that he needed to relax more between balls and develop a 'fierce focus' when the ball was released from the bowler's arm. Twelfth man in the first two 'Tests' Greg watched brother Ian leading the way, making 634 runs at 79.25, including four hundreds, before weighing in heavily in three matches with 425 runs at 106.25.

During the 1971/72 summer, Keith Stackpole, Ian, Greg Chappell and Doug Walters rebuilt their confidence, scoring almost 70 per cent of Australia's runs. The disappointment was a lack of new batting talent. An obvious example was using eight opening batting partners for Keith Stackpole over two years. Despite the previous season's axing, Bill Lawry remained the best option for the tour ahead, although doubt over the makeup of the middle order remained. John Benaud's 99 in the Adelaide international showed promising signs, but an unproductive Shield season cost him. John Inverarity's trial as an opener then all-rounder had moderate results. The fast bowling stocks appeared more assured. Lillee's performances were at times world-class, while Bob Massie's 7 for 76 in the first innings of the Sydney 'Test' provided a hint as to what he could achieve when the atmosphere was conducive to swing bowling. The spin bowlers struggled; Kerry O'Keeffe took just eight wickets in the Rest of the World series at 51 and Terry Jenner 10 at 34.

Graham McKenzie managed a season's tally of 43 wickets at 23.45, as Bernard Whimpress noted in *On our Selection.* 'A lower average than Hammond, Massie and Colley. Inverarity, who mainly existed on the periphery of Test selection as a batsman and left-arm orthodox spinner, was picked as vice-captain for one test against the Rest of the World in 1971/72 until pneumonia kept him out for the Third.'

Ian Chappell was relieved when Keith Stackpole was selected as his deputy. Stackpole had a calm temperament and could accelerate the scoring rate without a sudden rush of blood. Chappell knew the selectors would never choose the outspoken Victorian as the

Australian captain and Stackpole, keen to concentrate on his batting, didn't want the job. Chappell also believed that if Australia continued with its tradition of picking the team first, then the skipper, he'd be safe, at least for a while. 'I didn't think Invers was a good enough batsman to play for Australia so that probably helped me.' Chappell's uncertainty remained when Stackpole, as vice-captain, threw his wicket away approaching a hundred for the second time in the match against the Rest of the World at Sydney (he scored 485 runs at 53.88 in the series). Chappell rebuked him, 'Listen, you fat bastard, don't you like making hundreds? And second, don't do anything to give them an excuse to dump you as vice-captain.'

While Ian Chappell may not have been Bradman's first choice as captain, he defended the Australian captain when an *SMH* editorial in January 1972 launched an extraordinary attack. 'Based on his performance yesterday, Ian Chappell should not be in charge of a ludo team, let alone an Australian side bound for a Test series in England.' The editorial claimed that Chappell bowled South Australian leg spinner Terry Jenner at the expense of Kerry O'Keeffe and others to bolster Jenner's claims for selection on the Ashes tour, set a far too defensive field for Dennis Lillee, and delayed giving him the new ball.

As John Benaud noted later in *Matters of Choice*, the editor of the *Herald* received a letter from Sir Donald Bradman as Chairman of the Australian Board of Control in protest at what was written. Bradman defended Chappell's 'great record as a worthy Australian representative' before asking about the qualifications of the sporting editor of the *SMH*. It looked like Bradman's old teammate Bill O'Reilly (the paper's chief cricket writer) was loading the bullets. Bradman's response to the editor contained a reference to 'petty State jealousies' revealing that Bradman was ready to defend Chappell and that old rivalries (between Bradman and O'Reilly) die hard.

Ian Chappell knew the 1972 tour of England was his chance to establish his national leadership credentials. His job would also be on the line should the side fail. At times Chappell felt like Bradman was waiting for him to fail. 'If I'd had a dud tour and we'd lost, I could have lost the captaincy. I didn't think for a moment that I was a universal choice with the selectors. I'm still staggered I got the job in the first place, and I can't believe Bradman would have wanted me.'

The tour ended as Eric Beecher in *Australian Cricket* described, with Sir Donald Bradman standing like a 'working director' on the steps of the Adelaide Oval Members' Stand, coatless with his shirtsleeves rolled up in the heat of a 35-degree day, congratulating the captains of both sides and calling for three cheers for the victors. The tour, dictated by political, not cricketing, circumstances, had ended.

Despite all the great cricketing moments of the Rest of the World Series, one ball gained the most attention. It's an instant that sits uncomfortably in the pantheon of Australian cricket images. It involves Graeme Watson being poleaxed at the hands of an accidental beamer from Tony Greig in the Third 'Test' at the MCG. Watson instinctively moved to hook and edged the ball into his face. The bloodied image of the batsman being carried off the field was enshrined in colour on the cover of *Six and Out*, Jack Pollard's collection of writings. Watson spent two weeks in intensive care, fortified by 20 litres of blood. At one stage, he stopped breathing and was brought back to life. The specialist's advice was clear, 'Don't play again.' Like many of his sporting generation, Watson ignored the advice. 'I thought a beamer, not a bouncer, hit me. I'll be fine.'

Two months later, Watson celebrated WA's Shield win with teammates when he learned he was one of the six Western Australians picked in Australia's 1972 Ashes side. By any measure, it was an eventful summer.

Bouncer preparation and picking the touring side

Approaching the tour, it was obvious that bouncers would play an increasing role against the Australians. They had been repeatedly bounced by Peter Pollock and Mike Procter in South Africa in 1970 and then by John Snow and Bob Willis (an England find as a 20-year-old during the 1970/71 series less than a year later). Ian Chappell knew he and his top order were in for more short-pitched balls on the 1972 tour of England. In preparation, he spent the winter with his brother Greg, practising against short-pitched deliveries on a concrete pitch in the Adelaide parklands. They would pepper each other with baseballs, landing halfway down the pitch to practice hooking the ball. They both knew the hook was the best way to respond, having watched Keith Stackpole effectively employ it against Snow.

The early 1970s was a reminder that success in dual sports could be achieved. As an example, five VFL players appeared for their state in Shield cricket: Peter Bedford (South Melbourne), Max Walker (Melbourne), Robert Rose (Collingwood), John Stephens (Melbourne) and John Scholes (North Melbourne). Cricket and football seasons had yet to bleed into one another, making it impossible to pursue both sports. Meanwhile, fans of cricket literature – a thriving business in Australia in the early 1970s with at least eight local titles released in 1971 – would have been delighted at the news that the doyen of Australian cricket writing, Ray Robinson, had been awarded a Literary Grant to produce a book on Australian captains. The book, *On Top Down Under*, is considered one of the best cricket books ever written.

In February 1972, 17 renowned former players and journalists sat down to pick their Ashes touring squad for *Australian Cricket* magazine. Former captains Richie Benaud and Bob Simpson, Frank Tyson, Keith Miller and Norm O'Neill were among the experts. All bar one selected Graham McKenzie, 14 picked Ian Redpath, and 11 chose Bill Lawry. Miller was probably the most popular among former players because of his heroic on-field feats, wartime horror stories, and laddish attitude. He wrote sensationalistic columns syndicated by papers across the country. Miller wrote 'Aussies Throw out the Bores' about the haggling and discussion surrounding the selection of the 1972 Ashes side. 'A retrograde step' is how he considered the selection of Lawry. He picked Rod Marsh but described him as 'lacking polish and skill . . . a very ordinary keeper indeed'. It would be the last time anyone described Rod Marsh that way.

So uncertain were the selectors of the make-up of the touring party that they waited until after the final Shield game to pick the side. Finally, on 6 March, the side was announced. The captain was to be named a day later. When the Australian squad was read out on the radio, 67-Test veteran and former captain Bill Lawry, paceman Graham McKenzie, and reliable middle-order batsman Ian Redpath were missing. WA all-rounder Ian Brayshaw thought McKenzie was still a Test standard bowler 'who could have brought his vast experience of playing in England to the team'. McKenzie, who toured in 1961, 1964 and 1968, reacted diplomatically, 'It's bad luck for me, but it has been wonderful for WA, coming on top of the Shield win, and I would like to congratulate all the others who made it. I'm sure they will all do well in England.' McKenzie would play the season for Leicestershire. Brayshaw, himself a chance for the Australian side, thought the selectors were looking to youth, although 'the prospect of Lawry as a batsman in England must have been hard to ignore'. Brayshaw recalled watching Test matches in England and how raucously the crowds celebrated when Lawry was dismissed. However, by 1972, Lawry was 35 and hadn't featured in any of the Rest of the World Tests (despite his 5234 Test runs and having toured England three times). During 1971/72, Lawry carried his bat in successive matches with 116 against Lillee, Massie and McKenzie on a lively Perth pitch, and then 69 against SA on a turning wicket against Ashley Mallett (and scored 488 runs at 44.36). Perhaps Lawry's omission was the selectors wanting to give Ian Chappell a chance for his captaincy to breathe in his maiden international tour. The side was equipped with safe hands and lightning reflexes in the slips with the Chappell brothers, Stackpole and Doug Walters ready to snaffle any edges, and two of the best cover fieldsmen in the world, Sheahan and Edwards. The touring party comprised six Western Australians, five New South Welshmen, four South Australians, and two Victorians. The 26th Australian team to visit England was selected by Neil Harvey, Sam Loxton and Phil Ridings and consisted of Ian Chappell (captain), Keith Stackpole (vice-captain), John Inverarity (third selector), Greg Chappell, Ross Edwards, Bruce Francis, Doug Walters, Paul Sheahan, Rod Marsh, Brian Taber, Dennis Lillee, Bob Massie, David Colley, Jeff Hammond, Graeme Watson, John Gleeson and Ashley Mallett. The team had administrative support from two-time England tourists, Ray Steele as manager, David Sherwood as scorer, and Fred Bennett as treasurer on his second tour.

For Australian fans, the tour represented a chance to make amends for the 1970/71 defeat. Most would follow the Australian side's progress via newspaper reports, ABC radio led by Alan McGilvray, and twice-daily Test highlights on television hosted by Richie Benaud. Some wanted to follow the action at close quarters. Bob Cowper and Barry Jarman, both of the 1968 Australian campaign, led supporters tours. A large group from the Australian Cricket Society and Alan Davidson's 'Australian Cricket' World Tour also attracted a sizable following.

Chapter Two

The team

Ian Chappell

By the time the 1972 Ashes squad was announced, Ian Chappell was at the top of his game. The 38-Test veteran was fresh off a four-century summer against the Rest of the World, where he averaged 79. He had added to his credentials by performing with the bat while displaying astute leadership and popularity with his teammates. Chappell had already experienced success on his first tour of England in 1968, scoring 348 runs at 43, despite failing the following year in South Africa, where he made just 92 Test runs in eight innings. Aged 28, he was the most experienced player in the Australian squad, having accumulated 2219 Test runs with six hundreds (highest 165) at an average of 35. Most of his 53 catches were taken at slip when he took over from Bob Simpson. Chappell's quickness on his feet enabled him to score on either side of the wicket with a wide range of strokes both on the front and back foot. His more aggressive, brash and outspoken leadership style was seen as part of the modern questioning times, where players were more comfortable in casual wear than suits. There was little doubt Chappell was a players' man and a militant leader with a good instinct for risk. He symbolised the revolutionary 1960s in the northern hemisphere, arriving a decade late in Australia.

Keith Stackpole

Keith Stackpole, as vice-captain, was on his first tour of England. Stackpole was the great stabiliser, an experienced batsman with a

Collingwood working-class toughness. Popular among teammates and admired as a player, he was a good manager of people. Stackpole was the one who often took struggling players aside for a quiet beer to lend an ear and offer advice. His aggressive presence at the top of the batting order also gave his teammates confidence. His attacking style was inherited from his father, Keith Stackpole Senior, a VFL premiership footballer and state cricketer who had played under Jack Ryder. Stackpole's A-grade debut coincided with his father's farewell and the younger Stackpole exiting for a duck. Sporting lessons came hard in the Stackpole family. Six years later, as a 22-year-old, he played his maiden first-class match for Victoria against Tasmania, batting at number three, scoring 43 and 12 in his side's 196-run win. In 1963, Stackpole's pacey leg and top spinners attracted the interest of Prime Minister Robert Menzies, who sponsored coaching from Clarrie Grimmett. Stackpole remembered the move backfiring, 'Clarrie made me realise I would never be a very good bowler.'

Stackpole's first nine Tests were as a down-the-order leg-spinner, including 134 against South Africa at Cape Town in 1966/67. However, it wasn't until the Third Test of the series against the West Indies in 1968/69 that Bill Lawry unexpectedly chose Stackpole as his batting partner. Stackpole's swashbuckling approach provided the perfect foil for Lawry's cautious style. He was also a handy leg-spinner and safe pair of hands at second slip. He debuted for Australia against England in the Fourth Test at Adelaide Oval in 1966, taking two wickets for the match and scoring 43 batting at number eight in Australia's innings and nine-run win. When he next played an Ashes Test at the city of churches, he was ensconced as an opening batsman. In 1970/71, when Sir Donald Bradman entered the Australian dressing room after Ian Chappell and Keith Stackpole added 262 during the Fifth Test, the pair thought praise might be forthcoming. 'I didn't think you could concentrate for that long,' was Bradman's opening line to Stackpole, who had batted just over five hours facing 335 deliveries for his 136.

A little rattled by the comment from such a highly regarded figure in Bradman, it reminded Stackpole of the value of timed and sincere feedback (a tactic he would use to effect during Australia's tour of England in 1972).

Stackpole and Ian Chappell were a great leadership partnership. When they played each other in Shield cricket, they were often at loggerheads. They had a similar mindset, unwilling to give the opposition team an inch. But as Australian captain and vice-captain, they worked together like a dream.

By the time the Australian side was ready to depart, Stackpole was confident he could succeed in England. His spell in the Lancashire League for Ramsbottom in 1966 taught him that English pitches took some adjusting to, but once he found his feet, batting in England could be 'very enjoyable'.

Greg Chappell

Greg Chappell started his cricketing life as a four-year-old on his parents' backyard pitch at his North Glenelg home. By age ten, he was scoring centuries at primary school and later represented South Australia at the national under-14 schoolboys championship, having impressed at Plympton High School. Joining Prince Alfred College in Year 10, he followed up with a hundred (against rival St Peters) and an A-grade debut for Glenelg in 1965/66. A half-century in a losing A-grade final against Woodville stamped his class. In 1966/67, Chappell debuted as an 18-year-old for South Australia, scoring 53 and an undefeated 62 against Victoria at Adelaide Oval. By the end of the season, he had made 501 first-class runs at 35, and the following summer his first century consumed three hours (104 in 170 balls) countering Brisbane's heat and humidity and the effects of a poisoned foot.

When John Inverarity was picked to tour England in 1968, Chappell took his place at Somerset, scoring the first Sunday League century and taking 7 for 40 against Yorkshire bowling medium pace. A pair of ducks at the hands of Surrey's Geoff Arnold was balanced within months by two centuries against Queensland. Chappell toured New Zealand with the Australian B side before winning a baggy green cap for the Second Test of the 1970/71 series. Having come in to bat at 5 for 107, aged 22, he scored 108 in four-and-a-half hours, adding 219 with Ian Redpath, who made 171. Greg Chappell had plundered his last 50 in an hour. Failures in Sydney, Melbourne and Adelaide were followed by a three-hour 65 in Australia's first innings of the deciding Seventh Test. After sitting out the first two Rest of the World matches as the twelfth man, he scored an undefeated 115 at Melbourne, 197 not out at Sydney and 85 at Adelaide. The value gained from Chappell's experience playing county cricket started to show. His combination of stability and aggression in the middle order was a badly needed boon for the Australian batting line-up. His Tests against England garnered 243 runs at 34, indicating potential more than achievement. As well as being a fluent stroke maker and equally confident off the front and back foot, Chappell had razor-sharp reflexes in the slips, anticipation in the covers, and a fast and accurate arm. The tour to England would be his sternest test yet.

David Colley

For David Colley, being picked for Australia was a dream come true. The tall New South Welshman with the cheeky face and brown curly locks could have passed for a 1970s model in a Peter Stuyvesant advertisement.

As a boy, Colley curated a turf pitch in the backyard of his parents' Balmoral home for five-day Tests and, after school, he played three-a-side with his schoolmates. By age 12, Colley was playing with the seniors in Mosman's third grade, taking ten wickets in one match. He debuted for Mosman A grade as a number five batsman, and denied Australian and New South Wales opening bowler Dave Renneberg a hat-trick. Experience as a pitcher in the state baseball squad improved Colley's ability to gain lift when he bowled.

A bout of meningitis affected Colley's final year at school; he took his father's advice. 'You don't need to be bright to work in marketing, and you don't need a qualification.' Dressed in his school blazer, Colley scored a good job in his second interview. The boss was a cricket tragic and recognised Colley's name. By then, he'd been playing A grade for 18 months for Mosman and was included in the NSW practice squad training with Bob Simpson, Richie Benaud, Neil Harvey, Peter Philpott and Johnny Martin. But it was Alan Davidson's advice that stuck. 'We're all human . . . they've all got a bat and ball, and you've got the same . . . go out there and take them on.'

Offers to play in the Lancashire League were rejected as Colley began working as a junior trainee in a small firm, occasionally with advertising guru John Singleton. By 1969/70, Colley formed a new ball partnership with Renneberg in a weakened New South Wales side and developed a reputation as an effective into-the-wind bowler with a surprising turn of pace. Colley's attacking batting also saw him score 101 against South Australia in 1970/71, his maiden first-class century in 17 matches. Colley was more a steady taker of wickets than likely to destroy a top order, but he attracted attention the following season when he captured 33 wickets at 29.33. He could barely move when he discovered he'd been picked to tour England. As he lay in bed suffering from the 'flu, Colley's mother poked her head into his bedroom door and said, 'There's a bunch of blokes here who want to interview you.' Journalist Rex Mossop was among those who went to Colley's parents' house, set up his television camera and announced to the world that Colley was part of the Australian touring side. 'I had gathered something was happening when all these cameras were in my bedroom. I also felt some pride in beating my idol Graham McKenzie for a spot in the team. I was pretty buzzed by that.'

Colley's next challenge was to balance his budding advertising career with playing international cricket. His smooth talk enabled him to negotiate a leave of absence with a job guaranteed on his return.

Ross Edwards

Once described as 'the little fatso who made good', Ross Edwards compensated for any lack of natural batting ability by becoming the best fieldsman of his generation. An only child, he was largely self-taught. He developed an independence that helped him understand his skills and play within his limitations – his four centuries during the 1971/72 domestic season earned his first Australian tour at 29. On the verge of being dropped from the WA team two years earlier, Edwards' six centuries in ten first-class games (including from the previous summer) now demanded inclusion.

During his landmark summer, despite his heavy scoring, Edwards secretly hoped he wouldn't be picked to play against the Rest of the World, explaining, 'I didn't want to spoil my chances of getting a tour of England.' An accountant by training, he worked hard for everything he achieved. Using nudges and glances, he'd occasionally produce a more forceful stroke. Edwards wasn't a natural player but described himself as 'an honest tradesman . . . slow and steady no frills'. Edwards was also one of the first of his era to realise how much his value was enhanced by being the best fielder he could be. Preventing runs in the field was the equivalent of scoring them with the bat.

His father had kept for Western Australia in 1948, and Ross picked up his dad's affinity with the gloves. By age 14, Ross had represented his state under-16 side in the 1957 national championship on Sydney's malthoid pitches, taking time to adjust from the slower turf pitches at home. Edwards recalled, 'Most of the carnival was washed out, and I spent my time eating chocolates.' When he returned, he'd put on so much weight that his parents had trouble recognising him when they picked him up at the train station. A year later, Edwards gave sport away for 12 months because of bone spurs that had developed on his heels; he later took up hockey. When Edwards just failed to matriculate, his parents decided to move to New Zealand, where he resumed playing cricket, studied to become an accountant and put a priority on fitness. Edwards also met his wife-to-be, Lyndall, in Auckland. A move back to Perth saw Edwards join the Claremont–Cottesloe district club as a wicketkeeper, where he earned selection in the state squad as a second keeper behind Gordon Becker after impressing the selectors with his keeping to Graham McKenzie, Laurie Mayne and Ian Brayshaw. Edwards aimed to represent Western Australia at two sports (cricket and hockey) before he was 21 as well as completing a marathon at the Olympic Games. He missed the mark with two but was part of the WA hockey team that defeated Olympic champions Pakistan; his first Shield game for the state came in December 1964 in Brisbane, where he replaced Becker, who had withdrawn with chicken pox. Stifling heat dominated Edwards' first experience of state cricket 'drinking several bottles of soft drink during the lunch break on my first day keeping'. He missed Queensland number three Bill Buckle more than once on his way to 207 before scoring a duck himself batting at number ten. Edwards, who pouched four catches in Queensland's only innings, had become part of history; the match was the maiden first-class game in Australia to be played on a Sunday. In 1966/67, with Becker in South Africa with the Australian side, Edwards got another chance. Batting usefully, Edwards made four half-centuries with 26 victims behind the stumps. His career as a stumper ended after he dropped a twin ton-scoring Ken Cunningham before the twitchy left-hander had scored in both innings at Adelaide Oval.

'Our captain Tony Lock made it clear that my time with the gloves was up,' Edwards recalled. He knew he struggled to keep to the spinners and wasn't nimble enough on his feet or agile with the gloves. He vowed to become a specialist batsman and cover fieldsman. In 1968/69, Rod Marsh became the third possible keeper in the Western Australian side, although Becker remained behind the stumps. Edwards notched a maiden first-class century, an undefeated 117 against New South Wales, finishing the summer with 488 runs at 56.

Edwards' turning point came when he finally qualified as an accountant in 1971. A clearer-headed Edwards scored a batch of centuries for Western Australia, scoring 733 runs at 64, enough to secure a place in Ian Chappell's 1972 Australian touring party. The only sting in the tail was Edwards feeling compelled to resign from his new job. When he signed on just months before, he told the accountancy firm that 'cricket wouldn't interfere with his work'. Although Edwards thought of himself as 'little more than an extra in the touring party', it was an opportunity he didn't want to miss.

Bruce Francis

As a young boy, Bruce Francis loved staying up at night listening to Ashes contests on the radio. With his siblings Peter and Margie and all manner of cricket books around him, he waited for the Alan Davidson quiz during the lunchbreak. Cricket was in his genes; Francis' father Cass kept wicket to 'Invincible' Ernie Toshack during a country week carnival in the 1930s in Sydney. His Rose Bay family also had a strong sense of compassion. Cass was a Rat of Tobruk, and his wife was the physiotherapist who nursed his war-withered arm back to functioning.

Bruce joined his teenage cricket-loving neighbour Peter Alexander in backyard games. Alexander's influence was so profound that Bruce convinced his parents to name his younger brother Peter Alexander Francis. Bruce wore Forest Gump-like callipers at night and was prescribed built-up shoes for school. Neighbourhood cricket matches soon moved to the Dover Heights Girls High School playground. In December 1954, Francis watched his first Test match, later playing with or against nine players (Cowdrey, Graveney, Bailey, Tyson, Evans, Favell, Burke, Harvey and Benaud). When still in short pants, Bruce worked the scoreboard at the Waverley Oval before scoring for the club's City and Suburban team, filling in if players failed to turn up.

Francis became a favourite in the local press when his Rose Bay Public School coach, Neville Montacute, described Francis as 'better than Norm O'Neill at the same age'. At Vaucluse Boys' High School, Francis was coached by the former Paddington all-rounder Ted Gill and played on coir matting pitches in the local park competition. Gill had cricket nets built at the school and found funds for a bowling machine (usually only available to state and Test players). In his teenage years, Francis was so passionate about cricket and rugby league that he used only sporting vocabulary in conversation. School first-eleven cricket coach Warren Kneen encouraged Bruce to read the *Sydney Morning Herald* editorial to identify words he didn't know. Australian film director Peter Weir, also taught by Kneen, modelled his character John Keating (played by Robin Williams in *Dead Poet's Society*) on Kneen.

As a 15-year-old, Francis was taken under the wing of Vic Jackson, a former New South Wales and Leicestershire all-rounder who encouraged Francis to open the batting. A few months later, Jackson was one of three players from Waverley killed in a level crossing accident (Jack Fingleton's nephew, Waverley stalwart Peter Fingleton, as well as A-grade captain Jimmy Walker also died). The trio had been going to Parkes in central western NSW in January of 1965 to play in a country match. The next day, Francis remembered his feelings of 'not knowing what to say' when sitting next to Jackson's son, the captain of the Waverley under-21 side.

A week later, Francis debuted for Waverley B grade, scoring 121 before playing the final A-grade game of the season. He made only six but remembered the thrill of facing Dave Renneberg and appearing alongside his mentor Peter Alexander, thinking life couldn't get any better. A New South Wales debut arrived against South Australia at Adelaide Oval in Brian Booth's final first-class match in December 1968. Francis scored 7 and 36 in his side's three-wicket loss.

Francis encountered Lillee in November 1969, wondering why,

when rain intervened, the WA paceman ran laps of the SCG number two ground while other players took an early lunch of pies, pasties and soft drinks. 'Cricketers weren't supposed to train.'

Playing for Accrington in the Lancashire League in 1970, Francis became the highest run scorer in the club's history. While initially shocked at the wintery conditions, Francis enjoyed life in the industrial town of around 50,000, 30 or so kilometres from the bustling northern city of Manchester. Accrington, one of 14 towns within an 80-kilometre radius, was often home to wet pitches and a rough outfield. Francis, though, found great camaraderie at the club and among fellow Australians playing in the Lancashire Leagues, such as Mick Pawley, Neil Hawke, John Grant, Tony Mann and Terry MacGill. The season's highlights included Accrington's win in the Worsley Cup (Sunday League competition) in front of a crowd of 5000, a holiday in Scotland watching the Commonwealth Games, and backpacking around France and Spain. The following year, he travelled to England on a Chandris Cruise ship to play for Essex. He shared a cabin with a Roman Catholic priest who was a missionary in Papua New Guinea and the Somerset-bound Kerry O'Keeffe. Francis led the batting aggregates, making 1562 runs, including four centuries, proving himself under English conditions. In the summer of 1971/72, he opened the batting for Australia against the Rest of the World, scoring 10, 2 and 22 before a hand injury ruled him out for the rest of the international season. By February 1972, Francis was tipped off about his selection by an Adelaide journalist; he was in the touring squad for England. Francis kept the news to himself and waited until the night the team was announced on the radio before quietly celebrating at his parents' house.

John Gleeson

John Gleeson grew up in the small village of Wiangaree in northern New South Wales, where his family had moved to work on the Kyogle–Brisbane railway line. Later, his parents ran the local post office and telephone exchange. Gleeson left school at 15 to work at the Postmaster-General's Department, where he was promoted to telecommunications troubleshooter. Beginning cricketing life as a wicketkeeper, Gleeson became a leg spinner, borrowing his grip from mystery spinner Jack Iverson. As a 12-year-old, Gleeson had picked up a copy of *Sporting Life* featuring a cover photo of Iverson and his unusual grip. He then experimented with a tennis ball against a jacaranda tree on a paspalum pitch. 'If there had been no photograph, probably there would be no Johnny Gleeson in first-class cricket,' Gleeson admitted years later.

Gleeson achieved his spinning debut playing for the Australian Postal Institute when the skipper, the former first-class player and later Test umpire Tom Brooks, in frustration, threw him the ball. In 1965/66, Gleeson, invited to play for Gunnedah, took wickets against a Chegwyn side led by Richie Benaud, who raised an eyebrow when the off spinner with a leg-break action perplexed the former Australian captain. Gleeson prospered at Balmain, debuting for New South Wales on the state's western tour of 1966/67, a team with five former Test players captained by an enterprising Brian Booth. When Gleeson was made 12th man against South Australia, Sir Donald Bradman, standing in front of the wicket without pads or a bat, watched Gleeson bowl in the nets. Gleeson said later, 'I tossed a leg-spinner high so it would take a spin, and he came across to let it go, and it came back and hit him on the leg. He retired to the leg side, and I bowled a couple more overs, and we went back to watch the game.'

By summer's end, Gleeson was selected to tour New Zealand with an Australian second eleven as the leading wicket-taker for New South Wales after just five games. A bout of the mumps after the tour was so severe that doctors had to work to keep Gleeson alive. Debuting under Bob Simpson, Gleeson played all four Tests against India in 1967/68 before touring England, taking 12 of the 69 wickets to fall at a rate of one wicket every 97 balls.

By the time he was picked to tour England in 1972, Gleeson had completed a tour of India, South Africa and England four years earlier. Such was the mystery surrounding Gleeson's bowling grip that in 1968, Ian Peebles, an English spinner in 13 Tests and journalist at *The Sunday Times*, cornered Gleeson at the nets at the Nursery end of Lord's, asking for a private demonstration of the bent-finger grip. Gleeson's 27 Tests had reaped 90 wickets at an average of 35.

Jeff Hammond

The rise to the top of Australian cricket was as quick as it was dramatic for the 20-year-old South Australian Jeff Hammond. He was raised in the small country town of Owen on the Adelaide Plains where his father was the stationmaster. As a boy, Hammond, athletic and big for his age, soon learned to occupy himself playing sports in the 'whistle-stop' town consisting of a railway station, school, a silo and not much else. This meant throwing a ball against a wall to test his reflexes or heading to the local oval to hit five irons. Sir Donald Bradman's *The Art of Cricket* was the source of Hammond's 'cricket knowledge'. 'I learned how to play the cover drive by looking at the photos of each stroke frame and reading the advice. You learned to do things independently, and any mentoring came from books.' Hammond's mother spent hours throwing balls for her young son in the backyard after school, and predicted when Jeff was at primary school that he would 'tour England in 1972'.

Hammond was a natural at all sports. Such was the excitement surrounding young Jeff's sporting prowess that his parents moved to Adelaide to further their son's opportunities. They bought a delicatessen at Campbelltown, and Hammond's mother helped bring in extra cash by working at Myer's Emporium in the city. The Hammonds lived in a unit in Payneham in Adelaide's eastern suburbs while Jeff, as a 13-year-old, played A1 Turf cricket with the local club before debuting in Prospect's A-grade side aged 15 and 299 days. For Hammond, then a Norwood High School student, it was an era of extraordinary success, with Prospect winning six consecutive A-grade premierships. Former club and state opening batsman Reg Craig's coaching was crucial to the club's culture. Hammond watched and listened carefully, joining a bowling attack that consisted of Graham Clarke, Terry Jenner and Ashley Mallett. The batting line-up was also strong, with Bob Blewett, Bob Gilbourne, David Strudwick and John Ducker making short work of the small totals they often had to chase. Observing Garry Sobers (1962/63 and 1963/64) and playing alongside Barry Richards (1970/71) added enormously to Hammond's experience. Terry Jenner was the most influential of all the state and Test players Jeff Hammond played with at Prospect. 'Jenner was a genius in terms of his cricket prowess. He could get the message through sometimes in a very blunt way, but it was sometimes what you needed.' Despite playing four of Australia's five 'Tests' against the Rest of the World, Jenner didn't make the 1972 Ashes tour.

Hammond was at his wife's parents' house when the *Advertiser's* Keith Butler called with the news that 'Bomber' had been selected in the Australian side to tour England. 'We were watching TV, waiting for the phone to go. When it rang, I stood up and said, "I think this is it."' Hammond had been confident of selection since he ripped through the New South Wales top order at Adelaide Oval in February 1972. As he followed through after uprooting Doug Walters off stump, Hammond felt choked with emotion. Having debuted for South Australia as a teenager with a side-on action and an elongated sweep of his arm, he had now cultivated a late outswinger to complement his pace. Hammond captured 34 wickets at 20 when SA won the Shield in 1970/71 and backed that up with 31 wickets at 24 the next summer. Picked mainly as a chance to gain experience, time would tell how long it would be before he played Test cricket.

John Inverarity

John Inverarity, encouraged by his father, Merv, a chartered accountant and Western Australian cricketer, was schooled at North Cottesloe

Primary and then Scotch College, where he led the senior school side. He was captain of the first-grade side at the University of Western Australia, leading the team to premierships. He was the first in his family to attend higher education and wanted to make a difference through teaching, where he began at Guilford Grammar. Inverarity remembered the words of former UWA vice-chancellor Alan Robson: 'If you leave this university with only a degree, then we will have failed you.' Disciplined at juggling the demands of university and playing Shield cricket in 1963, he sat three exams on the morning of Shield games. During home matches, Inverarity would teach the first two lessons before going to the WACA to play, collecting the school work to mark and hand back to the students. Inverarity was lucky because UWA registrar and Chairman of Selectors Arthur Williams was sympathetic. After Inverarity was away for six months during the 1968 England tour, he moved to Applecross Senior High School, where department schools provided unpaid time off. Inverarity was set for his second tour of England, hoping to improve his modest returns from three Tests of 113 runs at an average of 18.

He was picked as the third selector on Australia's 1972 tour of England. He had enjoyed a successful domestic season, scoring 742 runs, but only 32 had come from his four innings in internationals against the Rest of the World. His left-arm spinners provided as much an argument for his inclusion as his batting (he had also just led WA to a Shield win). Inverarity heard the news of his selection while teaching at Scotch College. That night, he celebrated with his wife Jane, and his teammate Ross Edwards and his wife Lyndall. A Perth photographer snapped Edwards pouring the champagne. Inverarity's selection might have surprised some but not Ian Brayshaw, who observed, 'Invers had an extraordinary cricket brain. In terms of strategies, I don't think there was anyone better. His sense of planning and memory of opposition players was very sound, as was his technical knowledge.' The incentive points system used in the Sheffield Shield required a canny captain to negotiate fully. The change proved successful, with points rewarded for runs scored over 150 in the first 65 overs of each side's first innings and for wickets taken in the same period.

Dennis Lillee

Dennis Lillee had come a long way from the working-class Perth suburb of Belmont, having been brought up in semi-rural Maddington southeast of Perth. Lillee's first cricket memories dated back to his maternal great-grandfather, Jack Kneale, who was credited with taking a hat trick against an Australian touring side on its way to England. Kneale was an all-round sportsman and one of the foundation members of the West Perth Football Club. As a youngster, Lillee wore special boots to support his weak ankles and, with the help of his maternal grandfather Len Halifax (a boxing trainer and cricket coach at Jarrahdale), taught himself a different way of walking and running.

Lillee played cricket with his younger brother Trevor on the backyard lawns of fibro houses in the suburb full of council homes and quarter-acre blocks. Dennis' father, Keith, even prepared a backyard pitch for his sons and their friends to play 'Test matches'. Lillee soon graduated to bowling on matting and malthoid for Belmay Primary and Belmont High School. Like many others, he was inspired by watching Wes Hall's 40-yard run-up during the 1960/61 Australian West Indies series. He also loved watching future teammate Graham McKenzie bowl.

Lillee was a hard worker. His love of training, including wind sprints and long runs, was encouraged by his grandfather and Ken Waters, his Primary School coach, to develop a 'will to win and never say die attitude'. Former Perth grade left-arm pace bowler Mick Basile, who emphasised 'speed at all costs', tutored Lillee. It wasn't long before he opened the bowling and batting in the local under-16 side, facing his future teammate and opening batsman for Australia, Wally Edwards. As a teenager, Lillee made the second side for the Perth Cricket Club, playing on turf wickets for the first time before the A-grade selectors knocked. A raw, ungainly action from 43 paces that delivered speed was hard to ignore. First-grade captain Kevin Taylforth insisted on a correct follow-through, while WA manager Bert Rigg and former England quick Peter Loader taught the young tearaway how to focus his vision on the base of the stumps and work up from here, helping to adjust his length.

Four years later, in 1969/70, Lillee debuted against Queensland at the Gabba, picking up opener Sam Trimble as his debut wicket in first-class cricket. In December 1969, Lillee featured heavily in Western Australia's ten-wicket win against South Australia, taking 7 for 36 in the second innings. By season's close, having taken 32 first-class wickets at 22, Lillee was on a plane to New Zealand for a six-week tour with the Australian second team.

The arid conditions (due to a drought) meant Lillee bowled on largely lifeless pitches. In five matches, he took 18 wickets at 16 with a best of 6 for 40 against New Zealand under 23s on a seaming Napier pitch. The start of the 1970/71 summer, which saw him bowling into the breeze to complement McKenzie's down-wind approach, was a struggle. Lillee's 0 for 117 when Barry Richards scored 356 was both enlightening and deflating for the young quick. Replacing an injured McKenzie, Lillee's swagger returned when he knocked Geoff Boycott's cap off and later dismissed him in England's second innings for nine. Ten days later, Lillee captured three wickets in each innings against Queensland. Trimble (who Lillee dismissed for 2 and 26) described him 'as producing some of the fastest bowling he had ever faced'. With Australian pace bowling stocks in short supply (they had picked and discarded McKenzie, Alan Connolly and Ross Duncan in the 1970/71 Ashes), Lillee found himself in the side for the Sixth Test in Adelaide. Lillee made the most of the assistance provided by the usually flat pitch in taking 5 for 84 on debut.

In the Australian winter of 1971, Lillee played for Haslingden in the Lancashire League, taking extended unpaid leave from the bank. He'd secured a contract of £1400 for the six months but had to pay his airfare over. Despite being described in the club president's report as the worst overseas player the club had hosted, Lillee took 68 wickets at 13, with the experience teaching him to slow down and bowl more accurately. The foothold at Haslingden was often too slippery for him to bowl at full pace, but it was here that Lillee learned to make the batsman play at every ball and mastered the rhythm of his run-up, giving his bowling action a smoother look.

The following summer's WACA blitzkrieg against the Rest of the World (8 for 29 from 7.1 overs) showed that Lillee was special. Subtle changes to his technique were working, as was Richie Benaud's advice 'to straighten your run-up', helping Lillee bowl a more consistent line and length.

By January 1972, Lillee had injured his back in the fourth 'Test' of the summer at Sydney. Lillee was bowling at a little more than medium pace on a flat pitch when Ian Chappell chided him. 'Look here if I want someone to bowl leg spinners, I'll ask TJ [Terry Jenner].' For Lillee, the jest 'touched a nerve, pricked my conscience and savaged my pride all in one.' He stormed back to his mark, determined to prove his skipper wrong. Lillee's delivery may have had Gavaskar hurrying his shot but it stopped Lillee dead in his tracks with a searing pain at the base of his spine. Lillee left the field and was diagnosed with a muscle injury. Lillee missed the Fifth Test, took 0 for 119 from 19 overs against New South Wales at the WACA, and missed the last Shield game at home versus South Australia. The injury to Lillee meant several weeks of convalescing before later running and training with the Perth Football Club at Lathlain Park following an invitation from Greg Brehaut, a former teammate at Perth Cricket Club and Western Australian Football League (WAFL) player. He was given an embroidered towel bearing the Perth Football Club's logo and sent best wishes for the tour. Lillee's two official Tests had reaped eight wickets at an average of 24.

In preparation for the 1972 tour, former state swing bowler Ray Strauss advised Lillee not to rely on pace alone. He showed him how to vary his approach by using the width of the crease and varying his pace to regulate the swing.

Lillee had also learned from Tony Lock that a psychological game was important. 'Lock was able to gain a psychological advantage over his opponents. He was able to think a batsman out.' While advice had come thick and fast at Lillee, his ability to apply the correct feedback and ignore the rest held him in good stead to lead the Australian attack, when all eyes would be upon him.

Ashley Mallett

Ashley Mallett's love for the game was born when his grandfather took him to watch the Second Test of the 1954/55 series at the SCG. Colin Cowdrey was fielding at arm's length from the young Ashley and his Pop as they watched in wonder as Frank Tyson sent Graeme Hole's middle stump cartwheeling. Although Ashley's uncle, Bill West, played first grade for Randwick as a wicketkeeper and opening batsman before World War Two, his parents had little interest in the game. When he was ten, Ashley's family moved from Sydney to Perth, and he joined the Mt Lawley Cricket Club. Starting out trying to bowl as quickly as possible, Mallett, inspired by Jim Laker's history-making efforts against the 1956 Australians, took up off spin. Encouragement came in the form of club captain and former state batsman Alex Barrass inviting Ashley to bowl in the A-grade net. Ashley's father's investment in a copy of *Wisden* fueled a love of the history and literature of the game. Promoted to A grade at 16, Ashley's role as an opening batsman and sixth change bowler initially provided limited opportunities for him to develop. Invited to attend practice at the WACA under Test player John Rutherford eventually led to an introduction to Tony Lock, although little helpful information was passed on. A line from Johnny Moyes' book, *A Century of Cricketers*, describing Adelaide as 'a haven for unwanted bowlers and the staging post for England', stood out. Mallett's tale of perseverance continued when he travelled to South Australia to visit former leg-spinner Clarrie Grimmett, who conveyed a valuable lesson: the need to flight the ball above eye height. However, Grimmett, then aged 76, having watched Mallett bowl, advised him to concentrate on batting. 'I could play you blindfold,' he said.

A northern summer playing for Ayr in the Scottish League initiated an invitation to join the WA state squad. By then 22, Mallett decided to head to South Australia (along with Terry Jenner) to try his luck at the Prospect Cricket Club. An almost immediate promotion to the South Australian squad saw Mallett welcomed by Sir Donald Bradman, making him feel at home. He began his first-class career for his adopted state wicketless against a visiting New Zealand side in November of 1967, before taking two wickets against India two weeks later. Six second innings victims on a sympathetic Gabba pitch was followed by eight match wickets at the WACA. Ashley Mallett was known for his quiet approach, but under the guidance of Les Favell, he and fellow sandgroper Terry Jenner took 60 wickets between them. Mallett's 6 for 75 against WA in Perth, bowling South Australia to an outright victory, provided the icing on the cake and enough evidence to warrant Australian selection on the 1968 tour of England.

Nicknamed 'Rowdy' by Barry Jarman for his quiet demeanour, Mallett had begun to prove the sceptics wrong. Mallett toured England in 1968, taking five wickets at the Oval, while later capturing 28 wickets at 19 in a five-Test series in India in 1969/70. After a six-wicket haul in the First Test in South Africa in 1970, he wasn't selected for the remaining three Tests and felt the weight of playing under a defensive Bill Lawry, who under bowled him. With Ian Chappell as captain, Mallett improved as an attacking spinner, snaring 54 wickets at 19 during the 1971/72 summer.

A skilful finger spinner with acute control of pace, flight and bounce, Mallett used his height to his advantage. By the 1972 tour, he'd played

11 Tests, taking 46 wickets at an average of 25 and was more than ready for his second tour of England.

Rod Marsh

Rod Marsh's hold on the wicketkeeping mantle was so strong that Ian Chappell even asked reserve keeper Brian Taber, a more senior stumper with more Test experience, to help Marsh if he had trouble with the English conditions. It was as if Marsh was born to take the gloves. Enjoying being Australia's number one wicketkeeper meant all those summers in Perth playing backyard cricket with his mate Bob Johnstone in the Midlands family home were worth it. When Marsh's mother baulked at the damage to the family garden, the inseparable mates moved to the vacant block next door, where they prepared a pitch on which they played from dawn until dusk.

At 12, Marsh was selected for West Perth's fourth grade and was state schoolboys captain of a side featuring future test teammate Bob Massie. Bruce Francis remembers meeting Marsh at the carnival. 'The players wore short pants, and Rod's legs looked more like billiard table legs; they were so developed. It made some of us wonder if he was too old for the competition.'

By 1967/68, Marsh had left West Perth (where Australian squad keeper Gordon Becker stood in his way of keeping in A grade) and played for University. 'I went there to learn how to keep to leg-spinner Tony Mann, that was a bigger priority than studying Arts and teaching.' Guided by Inverarity and Jock Irvine, Marsh debuted as a batsman for WA against the 1968/69 West Indian touring side, making 104 against Wes Hall, Charlie Griffiths and Garry Sobers (after scoring a first-innings duck). Becker retired at the end of the season and Marsh became the full-time keeper. Despite the honour of playing for his state, Marsh lost money on teaching days. Remuneration was seven dollars a day and a $2.50 meal allowance. He would have happily played for Australia for nothing and practically did, banking $180 for his first five days as a Test cricketer at the Gabba for the First Test of 1970/71. Queensland fans were disappointed that local boy John Maclean wasn't chosen and booed Marsh's early fumbles. The hostility from the crowd was obvious. 'I popped out of the woodwork, got runs and took some catches in front of Bradman.' Marsh was ignored by Australian captain Bill Lawry when he arrived in Brisbane. Marsh told Mike Coward, 'Lawry was under pressure after the team failed in South Africa. I don't think Bill even knew my name. Perhaps he didn't want me there. When I played under him, Lawry spent no time with me and didn't welcome me into the team, which I saw as a weakness on his behalf as a captain.'

Ian Chappell, Doug Walters and Ray Lindwall were quick to welcome the new keeper, including him in a round of golf, beers and a meal. Marsh noticed the side's mood changed when Chappell took over the captaincy for the final Test of the 1970/71 series. Marsh and Chappell were closer in age, played golf and drank. Marsh also liked Chappell's sense of humour and his inclination to spend time with his players, spending his captain's allowance on the bar. 'He wouldn't let you buy a beer but I didn't recall Bill buying a beer and he was never at the bar.'

In the First Test at Brisbane, Marsh's clumsy gloves dropped John Edrich, Keith Fletcher and Basil D'Oliveira; not all were straightforward chances, but all were top-order batsmen. Ian Chappell had jokingly called Marsh Iron Gloves after famous US baseballer Dick Stuart (a first baseman playing for the Pittsburgh Pirates who was a prodigious hitter but poor catcher, nicknamed Iron Glove), and the press picked up on it. When the series moved to Perth for the first time, Terry Jenner observed of Marsh, 'He won't miss a catch at the WACA. And even if he does, you won't read it in the papers here.' Marsh dropped Boycott in England's first innings. Marsh recalled, 'Iron Gloves was hurtful as much as I know I'd been born to keep and had been since the age of eight. I knew my first effort wasn't my best effort. I think the English press tagged me with the moniker. I wanted people to eat their words. In some ways, it was perfect for me.' Marsh's memories of his First Test remain relatively fleeting, other than the Brisbane crowd and his sense of unease under Lawry.

Hometown crowds continued to jeer Marsh at the SCG, objecting to Brian Taber's exclusion. Marsh's pudgy, unkempt appearance and ungainly style didn't help his cause. The knockers were won over when Lawry declared with Marsh on 92 not out during the Fourth Test at the MCG. Marsh showed his naivety at Sydney when England walked off the field after bottles were thrown onto the ground perilously close to John Snow at deep fine leg. He believed England had forfeited the match. In Marsh's seven Tests, all against England, he'd taken 11 catches and three stumpings.

Bob Massie

Bob Massie was a Hillcrest School senior team member when he was seven. When his father raised concerns about the age difference, the school's headmaster replied, 'I know it's unusual, but please don't stop him. He is the only bowler we've got.' Massie's nascent understanding of swing bowling developed by directing a tennis ball denuded of half its hair at neighbourhood kids (when Massie bowled, the air would flow away from the shiny side, causing the ball to move in the air). At primary school, Massie was inspired by WA swing bowlers Ray Strauss and Hugh Bevan and spent hours in the library studying cricket books on how to hold the ball for an outswinger and inswinger and ensuring the seam remained upright. Inspiration was also provided by watching Laurie Mayne charging in with a new ball using the Fremantle Doctor at the WACA.

Former Australian player (and Mount Lawley Senior High School teacher and coach) John Rutherford took Massie under his wing and was a harsh taskmaster. He declared, 'Les Favell would have no problem dispatching your inswingers to the boundary. You need to learn how to bowl a consistent outswinger.'

Massie was picked in the Bassendean–Bayswater fourths before getting an A-grade game at 16, eventually taking 36 wickets at 21. In December 1965/66, Massie debuted for WA, opening the bowling with Jim Hubble against South Australia, but failed to take a wicket. He spent the following winter Saturdays bowling in the nets, trying to perfect his outswinger as he listened to WAFL matches on his small transistor radio. Bowling in the nets without a batsman was a psychological practice that took the batsman out of Massie's mind. He also umpired junior Australian Rules football at Mt Lawley High School to keep fit.

Massie's first job after leaving school was as a bank clerk, but ever-growing cricket commitments interfered. When he was refused time off to play in an interstate Colts carnival, Massie quit and joined an insurance firm. He added pace, greater accuracy and a bouncer to his repertoire. Returning to the Western Australian side against South Australia in December of 1969, Massie took four match wickets bowling into the wind in tandem with Dennis Lillee (who captured nine scalps for the match). Later, he ventured to the northern hemisphere in winter (playing for Kilmarnock in the Scottish Leagues), bowling 'three to four hundred overs, learning to keep the ball up'. Massie took 10 for 34 in one innings in his first season, equalling a 35-year record. He also trialled with the Northamptonshire second eleven but struggled on the featherbed of a pitch, taking 3 for 166 in two matches.

When he returned to Australia, Massie's job prospects were so dire that he considered moving interstate, following offers from South Australia, New South Wales and Queensland. Eventually, he found a part-time job as a groundsman assisting Roy Abbott at the WACA, and, later, after marrying his Scottish girlfriend Nancy Coulthard, Massie accepted a full-time job in public relations at the Commonwealth Bank. His five-match wickets against the Rest of the World for Western Australia and four against Victoria, where he bowled Bill Lawry twice in the same game in December of 1971, caught the eye of the Australian selectors. When playing the Rest of the World in Sydney, he took 7 for 76 in the first innings. With confidence riding high, he now knew if his wrist was positioned properly on release, the ball would come out of his fingers with an upright seam, increasing his ability to swing and seam the ball consistently both ways.

Paul Sheahan

Paul Sheahan had movie star looks and top-drawer cricketing genes – his mother's grandfather was William Henry Cooper, an Australian leg-spinner from the 1880s. Initially raised in Werribee, 30 kilometres southwest of Melbourne, Sheahan was strongly encouraged by his father (a former A-grade district player) and uncles to play cricket. The sweet feeling of a perfect square drive as a nine-year-old confirmed his love for the game. Although Sheahan's initial experience of watching Test cricket was dampened by Frank 'Typhoon' Tyson's devastating 7 for 27 at the MCG in 1954/55, he knew then that he wanted to experience the drama and sense of occasion.

When the family moved to Geelong for work, Paul won a scholarship to Geelong College (where he later became the headmaster). Success for the Hawthorn/East Melbourne under-16 side in the Dowling Shield team introduced Sheahan to one-time Victorian player and mentor Clive Fairbairn, who suggested Sheahan play for Melbourne Cricket Club (where he later became the club president). In December 1965, Sheahan debuted for Victoria against New South Wales at the MCG in stifling heat ('well over 100 degrees at nine o'clock in the morning and nine at night of the first day'), scoring 65 and 5. He narrowly avoided a pair against Queensland (0 and 1) a week later before attracting the attention of the national selectors with a chanceless undefeated 106 in just his fourth first-class match against South Australia at the MCG in February 1966. A phone call from the Victorian Cricket Association informed Sheahan he had been selected for Australia. When his blazer and cap arrived in the post, the newly minted 20-year-old went to bed wearing his baggy green.

Sheahan began impressively with 81 on debut against India at Adelaide in 1967/68. The selectors were hoping for better returns for the graceful right-hander after his 1968 England tour reaped only 213 runs at 26. A century (114) in the drawn Second Test at Kanpur in November 1969 reignited hopes that Sheahan had arrived as a Test player, but success proved intermittent. Sheahan played against the Rest of the World in the first two internationals, scoring 30 runs in three innings, two of which were undefeated. For all his grace at the crease, Sheahan still harboured doubts about his ability to play Test cricket. E.M. Wellings in the *Evening News* described Paul Sheahan as 'a batsman of rare potential seldom realised' after his relatively lean Australian domestic season with just 328 runs from ten completed innings. A teacher by profession, Sheahan hoped to capture the imagination of the English cricketing public just as he attempted to do with his students. In 25 Tests, Sheahan had scored 1261 runs at an average of 31.

Brian Taber

As a youngster, Brian Taber took to wicket-keeping as naturally as walking. Raised in Fairy Meadow in the Illawarra, four kilometres from Wollongong, a love for cricket was born at an early age. While his mother, Mary, may not have appreciated it, Brian and his brother Ron honed their catching reflexes by throwing plates and cutlery to each other as they did the dishes. Playing junior cricket at Fairy Meadow Primary and Wollongong High School, Brian's talent with the gloves saw him selected for the NSW primary school team for the carnival in Adelaide in 1954, where Australian keeper Gil Langley advised him to relax on his heels and become more proactive behind the stumps. With his brother Ross playing first grade for Gordon, Brian debuted in the A grade in 1956/57 at 16 after starting in the fourths, with a reputation of being well dressed and always the first to arrive at the nets. Brian benefitted from Bert Oldfield's presence at the club and his timely advice emphasising balance and the need to find a way to relax between deliveries. Working at the Willoughby Council in January 1957 as a building inspector in the Health Department complemented Brian's studies. The Taber family's move to Chatswood ended his three-hour return commute from Wollongong to train and play in Sydney.

Appearances for the NSW second eleven from 1961/62 led to a first-class debut for NSW in 1964/65 after the retirement of Doug Ford, who had played 63 consecutive games for the state. Taber became Gordon's pride as the first player to be selected for Australia on its tour of South Africa in 1966/67. Having played five Tests in South Africa, when Barry Jarman was again available, Taber returned to reserve keeper status until the final Test of the 1968/69 series against the West Indies. By 1972, despite being the most experienced wicketkeeper in Australia, Brian Taber was overlooked by Australian selectors since returning from the 1970 tour of South Africa. In 16 Tests, he'd taken 57 catches and three stumpings. He'd shared the record with Denis Lindsay of the most dismissals in an Australia – South Africa series with eight victims in his Test debut at Johannesburg. Despite captaining New South Wales to their best season for many years, he was again firmly on the bench.

Doug Walters

Dungog-born Doug Walters impressed early. He was promoted from the local bush competition into a New South Wales Colts side, where he scored an undefeated 140; one ball was pulled into the lake outside the Sydney number two ground. Inspired by the sight of a teenage Graeme Pollock scoring a century for South Africa during the Sydney Test of 1963/64, Walters, as a 17-year-old, scored 50 against a Queensland attack led by West Indian quick Wes Hall in 1962/63. When he made 253 against South Australia before taking 7 for 63 in February of 1965, it was clear Walters was destined for higher honours.

Two weeks shy of his 20th birthday, Walters hammered 155 on his debut against England at the Gabba before following up with 115 in the Second Test. He missed the 1966/67 tour of South Africa because he was called up to National Service but was discharged before going to Vietnam – despite pressure from army authorities to sign for another six months. Serving time in Vietnam, it was argued, 'would be better for his image'.

In 1968, Walters averaged 127 in two Tests against the Indians before appearing against the West Indies the following summer and plundering four Test hundreds while becoming the first batsman to make a double century and century in the same Test (242 and 103). Walters toured England in 1968 under Bill Lawry. After scoring 81 and 86 in the First Test, Walters failed to make another half-century. By the time he was bound for England in April 1972, Walters had averaged 54 from 32 Tests. Despite all his success, a question mark still hung over Walters' technique. His high looping backlift and habit of playing across the line made him vulnerable against high-quality pace bowling on seaming pitches.

Graeme Watson

Graeme Watson was a rare sporting talent, good enough to play for the Melbourne Demons in the VFL and Test cricket for Australia. Watson was on the football training track in the winter of 1966 when he heard the news he'd been picked for Australia. The previous summer, a second innings century helped steer Victoria to a three-wicket win against Queensland. An 80 playing South Australia and a six-wicket haul was enough for the Australian selectors to think he was close to earning national honours. One night after training, Melbourne's coach Norm Smith took Watson to the MCG change rooms. 'You should think about giving footy away and concentrate on cricket. It's a great chance to represent your country. An honour you couldn't have playing footy.' Watson was just 21. His 18-game VFL career was over.

Ian Chappell first met Graeme Watson during a windy and, at times, rain-interrupted drawn encounter at the Adelaide Oval in November of 1965. Chappell made a first innings 82, Watson 31. 'Graeme was an unusual Victorian in that he'd have a beer with you after the game.' Chappell later reflected they had a few things in common: a love of the odd beverage and a straightforward, optimistic approach to cricket and life. The two were roommates for the 1966/67 South African and Rhodesian tour under skipper Bob Simpson, and a friendship soon blossomed and stuck. Chappell admired Watson's hard-hitting style, nerve, and the way nothing much seemed to bother him. They scored their first centuries for Australia in tandem at Eastern Province at St George's Park in November 1966. Watson debuted at Test level as an all-rounder batting number eight in the Second Test at Cape Town, scoring a 50 in 95 minutes, adding 128 for the seventh wicket with Keith Stackpole. A turned ankle bowling meant Watson was reduced to cricket in hotel corridors on crutches with a leg in plaster. Back for the final two Tests, his 2 for 67 included South Africa's top order Ali Bacher and Tiger Lance in Johannesburg. Watson missed out in the final encounter at Port Elizabeth, where Australia lost a series for the first time in South Africa, but was rewarded with a New Zealand tour with an Australian B side in February and March of 1970 (after a scorching 150 in three hours against Western Australia at the MCG).

Halfway through 1971, he realised cricket couldn't pay the bills, retired from the game and moved to Perth to set up a series of wine bars and cafes with WA winemaker George Casellas. Watson had been in the West a few months when Rod Marsh and John Inverarity dropped by to see him at work.

'Fancy a game?'

He did.

Immediately comfortable in the black and gold, Watson took four wickets and struck 145 in 307 minutes against Queensland at the WACA. Watson walked after edging to point, but the ball bounced.

The umpires were instructed to record Watson's 'dismissal' as retired.

When some Western Australian players dined out in March of 1972 to celebrate winning the Sheffield Shield, Graeme Watson rang Massie to ask him to join them. Massie responded, 'They've just announced the touring side for England, and you're in it.' Watson almost dropped his beer.

Ray Steele

Nicknamed 'Castor', team manager Ray Steele was a Melbourne lawyer who realised that a winning team was a happy team. By 1972, Steele had long been a cricket administrator, complementing his double Blue at Melbourne University, captaining both the cricket and football sides. Steele played league football for Richmond, featuring in a premiership in 1943, and district cricket for University and Hawthorn–East Melbourne (HEM). Steele, a man of charm and professional skill, was the HEM club president and the Victorian Cricket Association treasurer.

Steele told the new captain that the side would always be known as Ian Chappell's 1972 Australian team. For Chappell, it was a moment of clarity. 'Here was a Board man telling me that it was going to be known as my team, and I think that just crystallised it for me that the wins and losses were going to go against my name.' Steele knew how to strike the right chord with the players. 'We were underestimated, which gives us an advantage if we keep tight as a group.'

Ray Steele gathered himself for a challenging five-and-a-half-month tour as the Australian team manager. When asked by the local press about the makeup of the Australian squad, he responded, 'The more I analyse it, the more I like it, for we have youth and enthusiasm, and it should develop into a formidable combination.' Steele compared comments about Richie Benaud's 1961 side and its 2–1 victory, and Bob Simpson's 1964 team when it retained the Ashes 1–0. 'I'm hoping for a hat-trick,' he said. Steele was an administrator who knew how to tread the line between authority and camaraderie. He could command respect and be one of the boys.

For Ian Chappell and his players, Steele was perfect for the job. When Steele told the Australians that canned Foster's Lager was breaking into the English alcohol market, they reacted with a roar.

Press reaction to the Australian squad

Just three players in the Australian squad were in their 30s; their skipper, Ian Chappell, was 28. Seven players were under 25. Nine of the 17 places had gone to batsmen when eight was usually considered enough. Eight of the side were unknown on county grounds; a ninth, Bruce Francis, had played one season for Essex and a tenth, Greg Chappell, two seasons with Somerset. The remaining seven toured under Lawry in 1968.

In the *Sydney Morning Herald*, former Australian leg-spinner Bill O'Reilly thought the side provided a look to the future. Similar reactions were heard in England. *Evening Standard* cricket writer John Thicknesse thought the attack was desperately thin, a lot was expected from a bit part allrounder, and that Lawry and Redpath would be sorely missed at the top of the order. Lancashire captain Jack Bond in *Playfair Cricket Monthly* predicted England would triumph but noted caution: 'I've had too much experience to believe that nothing can go wrong for England, and nothing right for the Aussies. However, it would not surprise me to see England win three of the Tests.' As selected players celebrated nationwide, none was more buoyant than the Western Australians. Led by John Inverarity, they won the Sheffield Shield by one point from South Australia in the final match of the summer. Ross Edwards, John Inverarity, Bob Massie, Dennis Lillee, Graeme Watson and Rod Marsh were England-bound.

Departure

Jeff Hammond struggled to fall asleep the night before the team's departure. Due to travel to Sydney to meet up with teammates, Hammond nodded off at five and then slept through his alarm. For someone known for his punctuality, it was a rare mistake. 'It was the only time I have ever been late for anything. I was meant to catch the plane from Adelaide to Sydney, where the players met at the New South Wales Cricket Association headquarters at 10 am, but I woke up only 20 minutes before the flight took off.' He may have been delayed a few hours, but Hammond couldn't wait to get his hands on his Australian cap, green and gold jumpers, and blazers.

The Western Australian contingent stayed overnight at the Wynyard Travel Lodge Motel in York Street, Sydney, waiting for their teammates to arrive. Bob Massie remembered the excitement of opening his gear bag: 'All these bags were lined up with *1972 Australian Tour of England* emblazoned across them and several brand-new baggy greens and jumpers inside.' The allocation was two caps, two pullovers (one sleeved, one sleeveless), and an Australian tie and blazer. The Australian side's heavier luggage had already been sent on the *Iberia* for pick up in Southampton.

For the next five-and-a-half months, the team's mail address was:

1972 Australian Cricket Team,
Waldorf Hotel,
Aldwych, London, WC2 B4DD, England

The 17-man Australian squad featured a range of occupations. Four were promotions officers (Ian and Greg Chappell, Keith Stackpole and Doug Walters), two were Postmaster General (PMG) technicians (John Gleeson and Jeff Hammond), David Colley was an advertising account executive, Ross Edwards an accountant, John Inverarity, Rod Marsh and Paul Sheahan were schoolteachers, Bob Massie and Dennis Lillee were bank officers, Ashley Mallett was an advertising manager, and Brian Taber was a cricket coach. Bruce Francis and Graeme Watson were the only full-time professional cricketers.

There was a buzz of excitement as the Australians made last-minute purchases before heading for a team lunch at the Menzies Hotel. Wives, family and numerous hangers-on joined the Australian side in the VIP room. After jetting out of Mascot Airport on QF 530 on a Boeing 747, the Australians experienced delays in transit in San Francisco. Most of the squad headed to a strip show before catching the midnight flight to New York. Paul Sheahan fell asleep in one of the plane's toilets and, on arrival at JFK Airport, was removed at gunpoint. After the side disembarked, Ray Steele received a call to present to Kennedy Airport's security department, where he found Sheahan surrounded by police. The players stood around in disbelief. In the end, it took some fast-talking from Steele to convince the police that Sheahan was not a terrorist.

It is worth noting that by the time the Australians arrived in the United States, more than 1000 Federal marshals were assigned to airports to search for and, if necessary, arrest passengers. In the first three months of 1972, an era of hijacks, there were 515 arrests, of which 103 were charged with carrying weapons aboard planes or being on the run from the law.

Chapter Three

Preliminaries

'Gee, I'd like to buy that whistle,' said a member of the press as Ian Chappell and Doug Walters walked out of the Waldorf Hotel on a cool mid-April evening.

So began Chappell's book *Tigers Among the Lions*, his account of the 1972 Ashes tour. 'Whistle', short for whistle and flute, was Cockney rhyming slang for suit. Chappell and Walters had arrived in England 12 hours before the rest of the side, the captain dressed in an Australian-made mauve safari suit more suitable for the heat of the West Indies from where he'd come than the English chill of an April day. Chappell and Walters had just played in a double-wicket competition that was also a testimonial for Garry Sobers in Jamaica.

Travelling on a BOAC Flight 500 via New York, they arrived at 8.40 am on 18 April. The pair spent the day resting and settling into their rooms before meeting the rest of the squad at Heathrow Airport at 10.25 pm. After the team landed, Ray Steele briefed Chappell on the plane incident involving Paul Sheahan. It was the first of several on the tour requiring Steele's delicate handling. Another challenge for Steele was locating the Australians' lost baggage. Keith Stackpole had to wear the same pink shirt and blueish-grey suit for four days. Many struggled to sleep on their first night at the sedate Waldorf Hotel. The new players looked on with wonder at the Waldorf's 60-metre curving facade of Aberdeen granite, complete with a frieze of cherubs illustrating the arts and sciences. Australian Associated Press (AAP) journalist Mike Coward may have viewed the Waldorf's as 'a pokey old place', but some of its finery impressed him. There were the first-floor bay windows with a clear view of Aldwych, a one-way horseshoe-shaped traffic way with its non-stop parade of cars, trucks, cyclists, black cabs, red double-decker buses and pedestrians. The hotel also had a gentlemen's smoking room, a billiard room, and large bedrooms, making life easier for the players who had to share. The Waldorf was in the West End in the heart of the theatre district; Australia House, Fleet Street, the Strand and numerous restaurants were nearby. In the protected confines of the Waldorf Hotel, the Australians felt they could be themselves. With his captain's allowance, Ian Chappell held court with a beer in hand and was always willing to shout a drink for those dropping in.

The more fashion-conscious Australians spent the next day in Carnaby Street trying new outfits. Given their lost luggage, a call also went out for shirts, socks, shoes and shavers as hotel staff checked the stocks in the lost property office, hurriedly washing shirts and repairing an electric razor. Ray Steele wore a shirt provided by the housekeeper and socks from the valet. Team scorer Dave Sherwood was sent to Southampton, hoping to get the bulk of the cricketing gear off the *Iberia* and back to London in time for practice.

John Inverarity, as third selector (who helped pick the team with the captain and vice-captain), was determined to deal with his role sensibly. He encountered the same pragmatic approach from Ian Chappell and Keith Stackpole. Inverarity knew he could work with Chappell's leadership style. Although more conservative, his approach would complement Chappell's 'charismatic, assertive, alpha male style that was consistent, positive and strong on self-belief'. Inverarity also understood that Chappell was well schooled in the game's history and technicalities. The pair had toured England together on that featureless campaign in 1968 led by Bill Lawry, but the world had changed significantly in the four years to 1972. The social revolution in Europe and the US had finally hit the cricket scene. In 1968, the Australians wore short back and side haircuts, black lace-up shoes, and grey and navy-blue suits with navy ties. By 1972, it was purple suits, buckle shoes, flairs, long hair, moustaches, sideburns and flowery ties – a very different social dynamic. Inverarity recalled that in 1971, the students held a strike at Scotch College, the exclusive boy's school in Perth.

'These were more rebellious times . . . that's how society was at that time, and that's what it was like in cricket; the team was much more flamboyant and rowdier.' The new Australian captain seemed to be in lockstep with the changing times.

Ian Chappell soon faced the glare of television lights, radio microphones, and pens on Fleet Street, deep in one of the lavish reception rooms of the Waldorf Hotel. His message was that the Australians would be taking every opportunity to win. Vice-captain Keith Stackpole didn't think much of the questioning from the English press, describing the event as a waste of time. He recalled, 'It would have been better to have held an informal cocktail party, simply so that you could meet the English writers and learn to know who, in future, you were speaking to if anyone tried to lead you astray.'

Stackpole used the chance to sound out who he thought might be worthwhile talking to and made note of some he thought best to avoid. Cameras flashed and journalists fired questions at Chappell and Steele, with the players arranged behind. Bob Massie was shocked to stand under the bright lights as an exhausted John Gleeson briefly nodded off, leaning on Massie's shoulder. Chappell stressed that Australian cricket was more robust than when England won the Ashes in 1970/71. His squad had at least three or four Shield season's experience. The press soon learned to appreciate Chappell's straight-talking and accessible approach.

Mike Coward was on his first tour of England with AAP in a group that included former Test opening batsmen Jack Fingleton (freelance),

Richie Benaud (BBC), Dick Tucker (*Sunday Mirror*), Phil Tresidder (*Sydney Daily Telegraph*), Graham Eccles (*Herald, Melbourne*), Alan McGilvray (ABC), Russell McPhedran (photographer, *Sydney Morning Herald*), Percy Beames (*Age*), Norm Tasker (*Sydney Sun*) and Phil Wilkins (*SMH*). The 1972 Australian press contingent was typical of its day; made up solely of men with a balanced blend of press and former players. There were no scripted messages from the players at daily press conferences via the public relations department of the Australian Board of Control. The media and players all got along, showing mutual respect. In 1972, off-field matters were largely considered just that, off field.

For the Adelaide-raised Coward, the tour provided a first taste of Test cricket. Having arrived in the UK on the *Fairstar* in 1969, Coward, basing himself in England, had been covering international sporting events such as the British Open (golf), Wimbledon, French Open (tennis) and Eisenhower Cup (golf), as well as the Johnny Famechon – Vicente Saldivar fight in Rome. These were golden times for Australian sport, with the likes of Evonne Goolagong, John Newcombe and Rod Laver.

Coward soon found his feet on the 1972 tour, helped by Richie Benaud offering his support and encouragement. It reminded the 25-year-old Coward that despite the intensely competitive nature among the journalists, there was also friendly support. For Coward, it seemed a long time since he had started at Adelaide's *News* as an 18-year-old before gaining experience in Melbourne for the *News* and, later, the Melbourne *Herald*. These were extraordinary times in print journalism, with over a million papers printed at 44 Flinders Street daily. In 1972, the AAP was funded by major newspapers, and its pressmen were the first to publish a story that would break the news or complement the specialist reports.

Ian Chappell rarely held team meetings and didn't believe in curfews. He knew his side was made up of adult men who wanted to play for Australia. However, at the start of the tour, he set a few ground rules, stressing that if anyone had a problem, they should come directly to him. His door was always open. When he saw Doug Walters smiling at this remark, Chappell amended his comment: 'My door is open until 3 am then I'd like to get some sleep.' Nicknamed 'Hanoi' by his army mates, as he was 'bombed' every night, Walters' night outings were legendary. Advised on the 1968 tour by an English doctor to stop smoking for a week to remove a chronic hacking cough, Walters calmly ignored the advice and lit up another cigarette as soon as he reached the Australian dressing room. Chappell knew Walters' laid-back demeanour often obscured a highly competitive and astute approach. 'A lot of suburban cricketers thought Doug was just like them, as he obviously enjoyed a beer and looked laidback. This couldn't be further from the truth.' The fact that Chappell was a drinker played into his favour. He knew that if he put his beer down at 11 pm and told everyone he was going to bed, it was a sign that others should do the same.

On his second tour of England, 25-year-old Victorian Paul Sheahan noticed a 'freshness, an expectation and youthful vitality about the 1972 tour that wasn't there in 1968'. On his first visit, he had felt less at ease surrounded by more experienced players like Bob Cowper, Graham McKenzie and Neil Hawke. 'I was a starry-eyed youngster back then, but in 1972 I was in the middle to top age range.' Sheahan admired Bill Lawry but noted the difference in captaincy styles between him and Chappell. 'Lawry's position was one of making sure the side was in a comfortable position before possibly going for a win. Ian Chappell was always looking for an opportunity to dictate circumstances, carried this attitude onto the field, and persuaded others to follow. He trusted his players more than Bill, which always yields greater returns from a team.' Chappell's leadership style was to collaborate and be collegiate, but all the players knew he would make the tough decisions if required. Chappell also had the advantage that his touring side was filled with young men desperate to make their mark.

Ashley Mallett thought Chappell empowered and trusted his players: 'He never questioned you or thought that you weren't good enough, so he'd make you feel that you were good enough. The other captains I played under were a bit different. He'd ask me what I wanted for a field placement. He'd go along with what you wanted to lay out as long as it wasn't ridiculous. He never told you how he wanted you to bowl (you never heard directions like "keep this bloke quiet").'

Ian Chappell also pointed out that he didn't want his players talking on the field unless there was something constructive to say – and if so, mention it to Chappell or the bowler. He tried to create an atmosphere among the team where if players had ideas, they'd go to him. 'When Australia was on top, the show pretty well ran itself,' Chappell observed. Chappell was also aware that you never know where the next good idea might come from. Despite his growing confidence, he knew he had yet to lead Australia to a win in a Test match.

Chappell had a welcoming charisma, and it wasn't long before people from all walks of life wandered into the Waldorf bar specially decked out for the Australians. More lounge room than a bar, the Australians often entertained the likes of Mick Jagger, dressed in blue jeans, sloppy joe windcheater and sandshoes, drinking a half-handle of Double Diamond, and Australian actor Ed Devereaux. 'Everyone gravitated toward Chappelli except a couple of Victorians who didn't drink but still mixed in well at functions,' Mallett remembered. Sometimes autograph hunters would approach and be given short shrift from the Australian captain (Ian was in constant demand and wanted to preserve some sense of privacy); his brother Greg could see no harm in taking 30 seconds to oblige and sign an autograph for a fan.

The Australians were also busy signing a thousand team sheets. Gone were the days when tasks such as this were attended to on the long, relaxed journey on a cruise liner. Ian Chappell had to be a diplomat as much as a Test cricketer and captain. The endless line of functions the Australians attended included time at the British Commonwealth

Society cocktail party, the British Sportsman's Association, and then the Lord's Taverners, helping raise money for the National Playing Fields Association. All were black-tie affairs. The Australians added a cheque of £1000. David Colley fondly remembered the functions the Australian side attended:

> There was a bit of whimsy from the players who had been through all of this. When we went to a function with Prince Philip as the speaker you'd think, Christ this is heavy stuff, and there would have been 1000 people in an auditorium all in black tie. It was an unreal atmosphere and you were treated with a level of reverence I had never been used to. They certainly held you in high esteem.

Early nets: settling in

There was a sense of great excitement on the Australian's team coach as they headed off for their first net at Lord's, with the newcomers lapping up the sights of the Grace Gates before pulling up at the steps to the dressing room. Under cold, clear skies, Chappell led the group across the turf, noting the slope toward the Tavern End and then on to the practice wickets at the Nursery End, passing the Middlesex squad as it trained. Stackpole recalled, 'A big crowd had turned out to watch us, and you could feel the eyes on you, assessing you and murmuring comments . . . You were on show among real connoisseurs.'

Wearing multiple pullovers, the bowlers moved slowly, allowing the batsmen to get used to the pace of the pitch. The conditions were new to five of the playing group as they sampled the pitches that dried the longer they practised. Dennis Lillee, wearing three jumpers and looking like Michelin Man, was worried that his back might flare up again. He'd taken the precaution of warming up in the dressing room and running three laps of the ground before entering the nets.

There's a photo of Ian Chappell and Keith Stackpole brainstorming. Stackpole is talking, Chappell is listening intently. The image provides a window into their relationship and the vice-captain's role. In the official team photo taken at Lord's, the 17-man Australian squad had four support staff: masseuse Dave McErlane, assistant manager Fred Bennett, scorer Dave Sherwood and Ray Steele. There was one vital figure missing. Daphne Benaud was secretary/personal assistant to Steele during the 1972 Ashes tour of England. She handled correspondence, requests for autographs, bat signing, radio and TV interviews, appearances at functions, attending sporting events (such as the FA Cup Final at Wembley, Wimbledon), photo shoots, and recording sessions.

Finances

Players felt the financial strain as the tour progressed, especially more senior players supporting families back home. John Inverarity sensed it, although he was not concerned. 'There was a groundswell, but I was never very interested. I saw my life as a teacher, a teacher who played cricket.' Journalist Mike Coward saw that as the tour progressed, Ian Chappell 'started to get edgy, irritated with a tiredness and sense of unease he hadn't seen before, as much about the length of the tour and attitudes of the counties who often rested their best players when they played the Australians'.

The more senior Australian players were justified in feeling frustrated. To tour some had to quit their jobs, others took leave without pay. The 1972 Australians were worse off financially than previous sides. For the five months on tour each player received a salary of $2650 (around AU$32,595 in 2024), plus a flat fee of $5358 per Test match, shared among the team members who played. The pay structure marked a change from a time when the Australians received guaranteed gate takings, being 50% of the gate provision. The new system was designed to give the host country a better chance of making money.

Tour pool funds known as gimmick or 'gimme' were added. Ian Chappell was the only Australian team member allowed to make public statements. Each time the side visited a factory, or was seen eating a sponsor's product or endorsing a product, a fee was paid into the 'gimme' pool. The fees though were small by previous standards. For example, every player from one team in the 1930s was said to have been gifted wall-to-wall carpets (rare and pricey commodities at the time), from a factory that only the manager and captain visited. Bob Simpson, who had an acute eye for commercial opportunities, believed the days of the real 'gimme' were gone by the 1964 tour to England: 'Before the war and immediately after it that sort of thing was rife.' By 1972, the gimme fund meant players could expect to pocket an extra maximum of $500 each, while the Australian Board of Control was predicted to take home a profit of $40,000 (close to half-a-million dollars in today's money). The relative pay of the Australian touring parties had declined since Bradman's 1948 Invincibles. In real terms, the AU£800 Bradman's men took home was worth more than the amount received by Ian Chappell's Australians.

Players often had to pay for their own gear, although some of the more enterprising Australians contacted sponsors like County Sports to arrange for bats, gloves and pads, creams, shirts and socks to be collected from Lillywhite's store in London. There were also bat makers at every ground with freebies, or offers of two bats for the price of one. Rod Marsh used a willow from County Sports, a pair of keeping gloves, and two pairs of batting gloves.

On the fifth day of the Lord's practices, Dennis Lillee decided it was time to build up to close to full pace. It caused immediate pain in his back and reminded him of the shooting pains at his last international at the SCG. Lillee tried bowling a few more balls but soon made a beeline for team masseur Dave McErlane, who recommended a rub down, a hot bath and an early end to practice for Australia's spearhead. The following day, Lillee was out early to do some exercises with McErlane. His back pain had settled. He tried a careful build-up to bowling his first ball in the nets, starting with a slow, medium pace, but was soon in pain once he put pressure on his back. Ian Chappell wandered over, followed by a bevy of eager press. Lillee moved away from the nets to do some fielding, keeping up the impression that everything was fine. Lillee, hiding his pain, thought his tour might be over. McErlane, ever on the lookout for player welfare, tried to reassure him. 'You'll be okay; it's only the cold weather,' he said, rubbing his back before sending him in for another hot bath. Lillee needed specialist help. He found it in Harley Street specialist Alun Thomas.

It helped that Thomas was a keen sports fan whose dry sense of humour and relaxed manner endeared him to the team. Thomas always met Lillee in the entrance hall of the surgery, before heading straight into the treatment room to keep the meetings out of view. Thomas, always reassuring, played a significant role in managing Lillee's back problem on the tour. Lillee, in his book *Back to the Mark*, wrote: 'On that cool day late April warmth came into my life when a relationship began which was to have a big bearing on the outcome of the tour as far as I was concerned.'

At least in the short term, Lillee's meeting with the specialist helped ease the fast bowler's mind. At Lord's, Lillee didn't attend practice the next day, forcing Ray Steele to answer probing questions from the press. Playing it down, Steele revealed that Lillee 'was nursing a twinge in his back and had gone to see a doctor'.

Another week of practice in London helped the Australians acclimatise. A nine-a-side practice match at The Oval delivered a faster pitch. The bitterly cold conditions continued while Greg Chappell and Bruce Francis dribbled a soccer ball around to keep warm. Ian Chappell reiterated to the press that the Australians would be playing attacking cricket: 'Trying to win produces the type of cricket that has tremendous crowd appeal.'

Arundel and beyond

Play began with a friendly 50-over match against the Duke of Norfolk's Eleven at Arundel, an hour's drive from London. It was a relaxed start to the tour at the West Sussex ground, adjacent to a castle and surrounded by trees with spectacular views over the Weald.

Alighting from the tour bus, Ross Edwards was struck by the breathtaking beauty of the Arundel ground and castle. The photographs had not done justice to the real thing. 'I could have spent a week here.'

'Is this normal for an English wicket?' a slightly awestruck Jeff Hammond asked as the players wandered to the middle of the ground to examine the centre square. The sight of the English cricket grounds filled them with a sense of awe and excitement. Ian Chappell reassured them that the pitch would be 'slow but true and much better than most private grounds'.

David Colley soon made inroads into the batting with four wickets and Bob Massie had the ball moving both in the air and off the pitch. Most of Australia's top-order managed starts after then uncapped South African-born Tony Greig had reminded them of his talent. The Duke celebrated his side's win by providing the usual aristocratic hospitality as the Australians retreated to the castle for drinks after play. The Duke's daughters were 'all unmarried, yet all so pleasant and good sorts', Keith Stackpole observed. The cold weather meant the Australians would have preferred a hot roast to the smoked salmon on offer.

On the cusp of turning 30, Ross Edwards was determined to make the most of every opportunity. Early in the tour, he and John Inverarity took a trip to Cambridge, including a service at King's College Chapel, and visited Fenners, where they watched the cricket briefly before retreating to the warmth of the car. They met David Prest, the former headmaster of Scotch College in Perth, for Evensong at King's. When they returned, there was dinner at the Savoy Hotel courtesy of the British Sportsman's Club, with speeches by the Duke of Norfolk, Colin Cowdrey and Ian Chappell. Edwards and Massie made their way to Oxford Street, where they sat and pondered the intricacies of the Underground train system. They marvelled at the ease of getting around the largest city they had spent time in.

Anzac Day passed with little fanfare, just more practice at Lord's and lunch at the Lord's Taverners, where Canon Laurence Jackson of Coventry wowed the tourists with his ability to speak without notes. Chappell had never before seen or heard such spontaneous applause from 450 people rising in unison and was relieved he didn't have to speak immediately afterward. Edwards was so impressed he asked for a taped copy. Chappell then traded his Australian tie for a Lord's Taverners one. A buffet and champagne lunch followed at the Sportsman's Club, where the players expanded their roulette knowledge. There were two more functions on 26 April, including at the Cricket Writers' Club. Hammond, a kid from a small country town, couldn't believe it. One of the younger players asked Neville Cardus if Victor Trumper was a slogger, which he refuted. For Cardus, it was as if 'some young music lover had asked me if Mozart had been a jazz composer for guitar and drums'.

The adventure continued on 15 May at the American Sporting Club with an event titled 'A Boxing Dinner Evening'. The unique format, a dinner followed by eight-minute rounds to help decide England's Olympic boxing team, was a novel experience for the Australians. After the first four fights, the Australians, seated near the boxing ring, had seen enough of the blood splattering and decided to explore more of the city before heading back to the Waldorf. A week later, the MCC held a dinner in the Australians' honour in the Banqueting Suite at Lord's. The following morning, a number of the touring party were up early, visiting the British Museum to see the Tutankhamun exhibition and lining up with the general public to buy postcards, wall charts and T-shirts to take home – the treasures of the Egyptian pharaoh that year attracted 1.7 million visitors.

Two days later, the directors of John Harvey and Sons Limited invited them to a reception at Harvey's Wine Museum. Ian Chappell's main concern was that he wouldn't repeat the same stories. England captain Ray Illingworth knew that attending so many events was exhausting. In *Spinner's Wicket,* Illingworth described his first tour to the West Indies in 1959/60. 'Approaching one Test Match, we had to attend seven official functions in ten days . . . there was nothing worse than having to answer a lot of silly questions from someone who doesn't play the game or understand it.'

With the players tiring of nets-only sessions, soccer balls were bought with the Australians getting up a good sweat before lunching at Lord's and taking the journey to Worcester.

As Ian Chappell stared out to the banks of the River Severn from the team bus, he wondered if his side would experience the washout, as they had in 1968. He was weary after daily practice and a flurry of social events. The steady rain continued for most of the 101-mile (160-km) trip from London. When the players settled into the Gifford Hotel on High Street, Doug Walters' concerns had more to do with hotel hospitality and lack of toasted sandwiches. Having asked for breakfast to be sent to his room, he discovered that tea and toast were the only food provided by room service. It hadn't changed from four years earlier when he had offered to buy them a toasted sandwich maker. Steele stuck a British newspaper article in the middle of the dressing room that labelled the Australian side 'the worst ever', pointing to it just as they took the field.

When rain caused the abandonment of the first day against Worcestershire, Ian Chappell, Marsh, Hammond and physio McErlane hit the local golf links. Other players moved around the ground, signing autographs before returning to the hotel to watch TV. Edwards and Mallett wandered around Worcester's streets with a tape recorder and camera, with Edwards providing a running commentary. As they did so, they smoked their newly acquired pipes.

Rain wasn't just following the Australians around England. On the day of the start of the new Benson and Hedges Cup one-day competition (29 April), rain lashed the country north, south, east and west, and not a single ball was bowled. Bruce Francis and Greg Chappell provided intelligence on the conditions. They were the only Australians to have played at Worcester, scoring centuries for their respective counties, Essex and Somerset. Having seen his specialist in London, Lillee travelled to Worcester on instructions to receive treatment from McErlane. On the second day, he felt comfortable bowling medium pace, but the pain returned when he tried to bowl faster. Orthopaedic surgeon Alun Thomas had advised Lillee he wasn't suffering muscular damage but rather joint trouble causing inflammation. 'You've just got to go out and bowl and, if it hurts a bit, just keep on bowling.' This was no help to Lillee, who retired to the dressing room to run a bath. Stackpole sensed how emotional Lillee was and comforted the sobbing paceman. 'Don't worry, pal; we're all behind you. It'll come good. You'll be right.' Lillee learned he would have to adapt and absorb the pain. Stackpole gave him the confidence to keep going without fear of being sent home.

Ian Chappell also provided great support, organising meetings with Stackpole and checking in. It was decided that Lillee would play the game against Lancashire, the second first-class tour game starting on 3 May.

When play eventually began at Worcester, it was only three overs on the second day before driving rain and light hail sent the players from the field in front of a crowd of around 3000 huddling in cars, behind buildings and in the pavilions. The rain cleared and Bob Massie, confined to his hotel room for three days with a cold, recovered in time to take six wickets in the second innings (ominously claiming four wickets from seven overs without conceding a run). Massie bowled well into the wind while John Gleeson restricted the run scoring. David Colley, who picked up Basil D'Oliveira's wicket, proved he was learning quickly by pitching the ball up.

Australia chased 130, helped by Stackpole and Sheahan's half-century partnership in 25 minutes. West Indian import Vanburn Holder eventually ran Stackpole out with a laser-like throw from the fine leg fence to the top of the bails. Having recovered from his cold, Massie helped entertain by imitating John Arlott's commentary and adopting Scottish accents.

The Australians drove through Birmingham to Manchester and checked into the Brookhouse Hotel. The accommodation was grubby and seemed even worse when the players walked through dirty, grimy smoke from the bus. To lighten the mood, Massie and Mallett made a recording of a 'Sir Samuel Smog' interviewing 'John Arlott'. Ian Chappell noted how the Old Trafford ground, which had been inundated with rain just days earlier, had dried quickly. The Australians watched Manchester United play Manchester City at the Maine Road ground, mixing with the players in the committee room after the game, including luminaries such as George Best.

Lillee under constant treatment and pain debuted under English skies against Lancashire. Tom Spencer, named as an umpire for the first two Tests of the series, officiated with Harold 'Dickie' Bird. After four pitch inspections, the first day's play was cancelled, meaning 13 of the possible 22.5 playing hours up till then were lost. Fourteen millimetres of rain saturated the ground overnight.

A choice of pitches was offered: one dry at the ends but damp in the middle, the other evenly wet. Ian Chappell voted for the former, and the umpires agreed. When play started, Stackpole (34) looked uncertain off the front foot but hit square with precision. Ian Chappell's 32 appeared the most confident before he declared at 6 for 161. Lancashire captain Jack Bond, who was critical of the tourists 'only using the match as practice for the Tests', closed his innings at 3 for 97, throwing down the gauntlet. Lancashire opening batsman Barry Wood remained undefeated on 52. Watching from first slip, Ian Chappell thought Wood was one of the better county openers. 'Wood immediately impressed me as a useful player, and I thought we'd see more of him.' Ken Shuttleworth, who arrived at the ground fresh from hospital at Congleton, where he had just seen his wife give birth to their first child, a daughter, took 4 for 38, accounting for Graeme Watson, Stackpole, Sheahan and Inverarity.

Lancashire, in pursuit of 222, had barely begun the chase when rain fell. Icy winds lowered the temperature to four degrees Celsius and mid-morning drinks comprised cups of hot soup. The Australians retired to the local cinema to watch James Bond's *Diamonds are Forever*.

Even at half pace, Lillee had struggled to bowl 14 overs, taking two wickets in the match. Bereft, Lillee lay on the dressing-room table while physio McErlane kneaded his back. Lillee then moped around the Brookhouse Hotel, where the Australians were staying. Jack Fingleton, former Test batsman now journalist, sensing Lillee's downcast mood, talked to him about his back problems as a player and suggested a few exercises that might help. The Australians then absorbed the atmosphere of being in a crowd of more than 100,000 at Wembley for the FA Cup Final to watch Leeds defeat Arsenal 1–0. For most, it was their first close-up look at royalty. They were seated near the Queen, Prince Philip and the Duke and Duchess of Kent.

Next day the Australians travelled to the industrial city of Bradford. They were struck by its beauty, its spacious parks and path along the river reminding them of Adelaide. There were rows of low red-brick houses with chimney tops revealing the edge of the skyline, and cafes, red double-decker buses, the ringing of the church bells, and bright little shops that stretched along Manor Row, North Parade and Tumbling Hill. With a soaked Bradford pitch, two unofficial 50-over matches with restricted run-ups were organised in place of the Yorkshire first-class fixture. Ian Chappell sent Yorkshire in, believing the Australians would benefit from 'seeing the approach from the local batsmen to the strange pitch before we had to come to grips with it ourselves'.

In the first match, Yorkshire captain Geoff Boycott was dropped three times as he peeled off a hundred with nine fours and two sixes. One of Boycott's sixes landed in the neighbouring Bradford Park Avenue football stadium. The bookies lost when they offered odds of 10 to one against Boycott scoring a century. Ian Chappell thought Yorkshire Richard Hutton's remarks from the previous Australian summer were worth remembering. When the Rest of the World toured, Hutton had described the wet wickets at Bradford, saying, 'Throw the ball into wicket there, and it sticks.' Ashley Mallett recalled Boycott batting 'like a man possessed in terrible conditions'. The England opener's eccentricities and search for perfection were on display. When Boycott edged past slip to third man, he ran down the pitch, yelling, 'Nowt off the edge; I turned face.' Boycott was ahead of his times in fitness, nutrition and fielding, but needed constant reassurance, something his England captain Ray Illingworth found himself having to provide.

Cricket mattered more to Boycott than anything else in life. Many thought him selfish. Former Australian wicketkeeper Barry Jarman, who played against Boycott in 1968, thought Boycott 'too selfish to be part of a team sport'. The example is often given of him working out how to play Australia's mystery spinner John Gleeson during the 1970/71 series and keeping it to himself. During the Third Test at Sydney, John Edrich, batting with him, wandered down the pitch. 'I've finally worked out how to play Gleeson,' Edrich confided. Edrich established that despite the apparent finger flick of Gleeson's bowling action, he rarely turned the ball. 'I worked Gleeson out two Tests ago, but don't tell those boogers back in the dressing room,' was Boycott's response. That summer, Boycott often discussed his teammate's weaknesses with Rod Marsh after play when they downed their allocated long neck of beer. Marsh drank most of Boycott's beer and took in his cricketing insights.

Australia only batted 17 overs in its first one-dayer against Yorkshire. The next day Ian Chappell half-jokingly suggested to Boycott that

Australia bat first, given that they had missed out on their overs in the first limited-overs match.

'You won the toss yesterday and could have batted first. Let's go and toss,' Boycott replied. Chappell called incorrectly, and Australia was in the field again. The heavens opened up, and the Australians missed an opportunity to play on a wet northern pitch.

When they arrived in Nottingham, some Australians walked around Nottingham Castle; others wandered the town to stock up on supplies before settling into the Derby Road Strathdon Hotel. When Lillee tried to bowl quickly at a late afternoon practice session the sharp back pain returned. Then, suddenly, a transformation. He woke feeling sprightlier and sprang out of bed for the first time on tour, only to have a sharp shooting pain interrupt his net session. 'It was like being dumped by a wave in the surf . . . one minute you're riding high, the next you're underneath the whole weight of it . . . things were becoming desperate.'

Changeable weather greeted the Australians, who scored 270 in 300 minutes. In response to Nottinghamshire's 176, Greg Chappell displayed good form for the first time on tour, making an undefeated 83 while Sheahan scored 69. Edwards (38) countered Notts' number-one seamer Barry Stead's tight bowling before edging to wicketkeeper David Pullan. Jeff Hammond's 5 for 46 tightened the race between him and Colley for a place in the First Test.

On return to London, Lillee generated some lively pace in the nets for the first time. 'That was a breakthrough day for me because I had bowled quickly, although it still hurt a lot. I was on cloud nine . . . or on the way there.' Lillee ran the surrounding streets as the Australians took on Surrey at The Oval. Rod Marsh became the third of the Australians to score a half-century (58) by mid-May, a reminder of how few opportunities the tourists had to score runs (as a comparison, Bradman scored 1000 runs in May 1930 while on tour). Australia limped to 180 against a strong Surrey attack containing Geoff Arnold,

Robin Jackman, Pat Pocock and Intikhab Alam. Ian Chappell was starting to wonder if there had been too many slog matches because of rain interruptions when the top order fell to loose strokes. John Edrich, on the cusp of turning 35, showed the Australians how to play a seaming pitch by making 110 and providing Surrey with a lead of 120. Ian Chappell thought it was one of the best innings he had seen from Edrich, with one enormous six off John Inverarity sailing through a window in a committee room, shattering the glass and sending the clerical staff running. Colley built up some pace for the first time on tour by taking 5 for 72.

Ross Edwards, rested for the game, spent the day at Hyde Park at the Speaker's Corner to listen to speeches and debates with Lillee and Massie, before opening a bank account for the team fund with John Gleeson. Chappell was happy to allow players free time when they weren't playing, realising it was one of the keys to surviving a long tour. On the final day of the match against Surrey, the Australian skipper notched up the first hundred of the tour (101 in 165 minutes) hitting Pakistan captain and leg-spinner Intikhab Alam for 25 runs in two successive overs. In addition, Bruce Francis (57 in 197 minutes) provided a glimpse of the form that helped him score 1578 runs for Essex the previous year, and Walters' quick-fire 42 bettered his first innings duck (the local press accused him of performing a 'wild village yahoo' when he was bowled in the second innings by Intikhab. Ray Steele humorously defended Walters by describing the wayward stroke as 'an attempted lofted drive forced on Walters by the ball dropping quickly in flight'). Rain again intervened to end the match with Australia 6 for 281. Of the possible 87 playing hours on tour, 41 were lost through rain.

The 1972 Australians were musically minded. As the tour bus chugged along to its destination a cassette player belted out Elton John's 'Crocodile Rock', Don McLean's 'American Pie', and Billy Thorpe and the Aztecs 'Most People I Know' – even Helen Reddy's 'I

Am Woman' was on the playlist. When they travelled to Hampshire, the South Australians in the touring party were looking forward to the chance to meet up with and play against Barry Richards, who had helped them win the Shield two years earlier. The Western Australians perhaps less so, with the 356 he had scored at the WACA still in their minds.

Even on a slightly damp and slow pitch, Richards scored an effortless and quick-fire 73. However, it was the young left-hander David Turner's 131 that had the Australians talking. Turner, who played with virtually no backlift, handled Dennis Lillee well in Hampshire's 311. Lillee's 2 for 66 off 16 overs didn't reflect his ease in moving for the first time on the tour. Inverarity's left-arm orthodox spinners netted him 5 for 67 and showed his skills could be helpful on a slow wicket. But if it hadn't been for Ross Edwards' 69, Australia's total against one of the weakest county attacks would have been less than 100. As it was they were dismissed for 191. Bob Herman, twice rejected by Middlesex, took four wickets. Tom Mottram, the only non-contracted player in the team, took three wickets, while John Rice, playing in his first match since a cartilage operation, took two wickets, including that of the Australian captain for just 12.

The best news was that in the second innings Lillee found a rhythm for the first time on tour as he took care of the first-innings centurion Turner, bowling him for 22. After the match, Lillee skolled an entire jug of beer in celebration that he had made it through the game unscathed. Ian Chappell recalled, 'It was a light-bulb moment when he picked up that jug of beer and downed it. I think Dennis knew then that he could overcome the injury worries he'd experienced earlier in the tour. Although we didn't know it then, in his mind, he knew he was back.'

Stackpole took Edwards, Colley and Lillee out to tea, stressing the time was ripe 'to start serious concentration'. Australian batsmen finally found their feet in the second innings when Stackpole and

Watson each scored hundreds, reaching 1 for 306 in four hours. Replacing an ill John Inverarity at the top of the order, Watson struggled early but cut loose, outscoring Stackpole (119 not out) in barnstorming his way to 176. In his syndicated column, Richie Benaud observed Ian Chappell's emergence as a captain. 'The most important piece of Chappell's captaincy comes shortly when he has to make a declaration instead of accepting one. It was enough to wipe the prices off the bookmakers' board and a few patronising smiles Chappell's Australians faced leading into the First Test.'

Illingworth wrote in the *Sunday Times*: 'So the man DID mean bright cricket', about Ian Chappell's aggressive approach against Hampshire. Stackpole saw the Hampshire match as the turning point for the Australians on tour. 'As we took the coach back from Southampton to London, a jovial mood burst out, revealing a confidence that hadn't been there before.'

The Australians weren't the only ones frustrated by rain interruptions. The John Player League had 17 of the 30 matches scheduled in May reduced by rain. Sunday BBC 2 viewers were incredibly unlucky. In the first three years of the competition, only one match had been completely washed out. Two of this summer's first televised matches were abandoned without a ball bowled. The players were also duped as none of the four televised matches started on time, and no batsman qualified for the £250 award for the fastest 50. When Australia played the MCC at Lord's, the game was supposed to double as a test trial. However, Surrey withdrew Edrich and Roope, and Sussex withdrew Greig, so they could play for their county (indicating the power of the county boards).

Now nearing full fitness, Lillee was struggling with the front foot law, no balling seven times in the MCC's first innings, making it 35 times he'd overstepped the mark on tour. Despite this, Lillee soon did a victory dance after trapping Boycott lbw for two. Still at least a yard short of top pace, Lillee made the MCC batsmen hurry their strokes.

Only the occasional Lillee delivery had extra pace, but the increase in speed was disconcerting.

Another concern was that Massie left the ground in great pain after bowling only ten balls in the MCC's first innings, confirmation of the niggles he felt when he played two one-day matches against Yorkshire at Bradford. It was doubly disappointing as Massie looked forward to getting his hands on the Duke ball with the more prominent seam used in England. Helped off the ground by Ross Edwards, Massie was placed on a table in the Australian dressing room where orthopaedic surgeon Bill Tucker examined him. It was fortunate for the Australians that Tucker was at Lord's in case of a further mishap to Lillee. Tucker gave Massie a pain-killing injection before diagnosing a severe abdominal strain. The injury for Massie felt 'like a knife being thrust into his left side'.

The spinners held sway, with Ashley Mallett mopping up the MCC tail, taking 5 for 61, and Inverarity's suffocating left armers netting 3 for 35 from 19 overs. Ray Illingworth accused the Australians of peppering the MCC batsman with colourful language. He thought that even the composed Inverarity was trying it on until Illingworth laughed out loud and said, 'That's just not you, John.'

Ross Edwards was learning that playing under Ian Chappell was a unique experience. Fielding in the covers when England batted in the first innings, Edwards noticed Mike Denness hitting the ball squarer on the offside down the slope toward the Lord's Tavern. At the time, Edwards was the only fieldsman in front of the wicket on the off side.

'Why don't you put me squarer at point?' Edwards asked as he approached Ian Chappell at a change of over. The Australian captain was quick to respond.

'If you think you should go squarer, then bloody well go squarer. You're the cover specialist on the team. I have a few other things to consider besides looking after you. You're an Australian cricketer now.'

Edwards panicked, worrying his tour was over, but realised that his captain, while blunt, was indicating he had complete trust in him. Edwards moved like lightning in the covers and now felt confident he could position himself as he saw fit. Chappell expected his players to think for themselves. Edwards was used to playing for WA under Inverarity, who was specific in his field placements. 'It was the first time I started thinking for myself on a cricket field,' Edwards reflected.

On the Sunday of the match against the MCC, Ian Chappell joined Ray Steele for a round at the Berkshire Golf Club, 50 kilometres out of London. Matched against Gubby Allen and MCC secretary Billy Griffith, the Australians met Second World War flying ace Douglas Bader, who, despite having both legs amputated following a 1930s plane crash, flew Spitfires during the Battle of Britain and made his way around the course refusing to use a motorised buggy.

In the MCC's second innings, Bruce Francis juggled before taking a catch from John Jameson off Lillee. Francis was rarely confident in the field and felt the pressure of playing for Australia. Illingworth declared MCC's second innings at 4 for 178, setting Australia 191 to win in just over two hours. Ian Chappell told his team to be positive in the Lord's change rooms. 'If we don't accept this challenge, we may as well head to Bristol [the next venue].' A previously grinding game was transformed when Australia thrashed 195 runs in 135 minutes to win with four wickets to spare.

The *Daily Express*'s Crawford White penned, 'Merry Australians smashed MCC's Test triallists to a dramatic last over defeat in one of gayest batting blitzes ever staged'. Both captains had set the template of attacking cricket. Graeme Watson gained confidence after his dynamic knock against Hampshire, and the team began building in confidence. Watson recalled, 'Collectively, we were playing a good brand of cricket.'

As the Australian tour coach made its way to Bristol, Ian Chappell noticed that the team was enjoying itself, a sign the players were building confidence and trust in each other. Ashley Mallett recalled,

'Chappelli empowered you. He trusted you and never questioned you or gave any hint that he thought that you weren't good enough.'

Greg Chappell had played at the Bristol ground during his two seasons with Somerset and warned his teammates that there was unlikely to be much play once that rain set in. Despite this, Colley revealed his ability to bowl both into and with the wind to capture 5 for 27, including the wickets of Test players Mike Procter and Zaheer Abbas. Hammond, who opened downwind, also bowled well, while Greg Chappell's curly medium pacers often beat the bat. 'Here we bloody go again,' the younger Chappell announced as another ball flew past the outside edge.

Having started bowling leg spin, Greg Chappell had developed into a more than useful medium pacer on seaming English pitches. He would have had another wicket if brother Ian held on to a chance from former England keeper Roy Swetman. After play, Colley approached Ian Chappell and announced, 'I can bowl fast if you need it.' The Australian skipper carefully made a note of it.

The Australians were relieved when the day was called off. Arctic conditions forced most to wear singlets and sleeveless and long-sleeved jumpers. With only four-and-a-half hours of play possible during the first two days, and none on the third day, the Australians played more golf than cricket. Ian Chappell, Brian Taber, Doug Walters, former England dual international Arthur Milton and Gloucestershire skipper Tony Brown headed to the local course near the British Aircraft Corporation Establishment where the Concorde was being developed. Playing nine holes, they were back in time for the mid-afternoon resumption at Bristol.

That night the Australians watched a benefit cabaret arranged for former England off-spinner David Allen. They met with former Australian Test medium pacer and footballer Neil Hawke (then playing for East Lancashire), who travelled with his wife Elsa to watch the match. Quick-witted Hawke was an entertaining raconteur, and he made the players feel at home.

Next stop for the Australians was Swansea, where Glamorgan was seeking a hat trick of wins against Australia, having defeated them in 1964 and 1968. Tony Lewis immediately sent Australia in on another damp surface, with Watson and Stackpole struggling against the medium pace of David Williams, who Ian Chappell thought was more of a grade bowler than a first-class cricketer. It didn't stop Williams blitzing the Australians, taking 5 for 31, including the Australian captain for eight. Walters contributed 47, his highest score for the tour. His partnership of 66 with Inverarity added in even time helped Australia reach 191.

Ian Chappell was also worried by back pain, exacerbated by the continual cold weather. His decision to exercise in his room to loosen his back made it worse, which he thought contributed to his first innings mistimed hook to fine leg. During a night of entertainment at the Pontarddulais Rugby Club, the Australians joined in the singing on stage. Off spinner Ashley Mallett led the way as they bellowed a version of 'Tie me kangaroo down sport'. The sound might have been a little unpleasant on Welsh ears, but the crooners were rewarded with a club tie. Mike Coward revealed his vocal skills by singing 'Moon River' and 'I Did It My Way', bringing the house down. A testimonial for Glamorgan's Alan Jones at a local nightclub had Coward, by invitation, performing again. When Coward returned to his table, he was invited to sing again at the next night's dance hall. Given the quality of Coward's baritone voice, it was no great surprise.

Glamorgan was quickly reduced to 3 for 7, with West Indian Test players Roy Fredericks, Alan Jones, and captain Tony Lewis the early victims. Rain washed out the second day, and Lewis declared at 5 for 93, enabling the tourists to have some batting practice. Jeff Hammond was learning that bowling short of a length and nipping the ball back off the seam had value. He'd also established that his bouncer, while effective in Australia, was less useful in England.

Watson's second inning 54 included two sixes before he was yorked by Roger Davis. Ian Chappell closed Australia's second innings at 3 for

158, leaving Glamorgan 257 to chase in just over three hours. As the second over began, drizzling rain turned into a torrent. John Inverarity organised for some of the Australian squad to visit Loughborough Technical College, which specialises in Physical Education. There, they enjoyed an indoor net and played soccer before watching the European Cup Final on TV. June heralded warmer days, but Massie, struggling with injuries, missed the next match against Derbyshire.

Bruce Francis was a complex character. Standing at 190 cm and cherub-faced, he looked more like a farmer than a Test cricketer. Indeed, he was a deep thinker and a graduate in Economics from Sydney University. Francis was introspective but companionable. Prone to self-doubt, he was a strong back-foot player who had played well for Essex the previous English summer. Hopes were raised that Australia had found an opening batting partner for Stackpole when Francis struck form with 117 at Chesterfield, despite taking 80 minutes to score a boundary. Initially tentative, apart from two half-centuries at Lord's and a second innings 57 against Surrey, his returns before Derby were slim. However, an unbeaten fourth-wicket stand of 106 between Francis and Walters (109) bolstered the Australians after three wickets fell for 73. At one stage, the pair smashed 50 runs in seven overs.

David Colley's first three wickets in Derbyshire's innings helped his Test chances, taking his tour tally to 17, and making him the leading Australian wicket-taker. Colley overheard Alan McGilvray on the ABC saying he was a big chance to play in the Old Trafford Test. A few days later, Ian Chappell gave him the nod. 'We are looking for you to open the bowling,' the skipper told Colley, who described it as a 'wow moment'; like news being passed down from Caesar.

Excitement was hard to contain. 'I was a mumbling wreck for a couple of days and didn't know what to do. I think he (Chappell) wanted me to prepare myself, so I did some more work before the Test.'

Keith Stackpole was struggling to adjust to the conditions, failing to reach 35 in a first-class match on tour. He lasted against Derbyshire until the third over when he edged Mike Hendrick to Mike Page at second slip. Ross Edwards, caught off a no ball from the first delivery, reached a streaky 23, struggling against the spinners. Nursing a back injury, Edwards believed, 'There goes my Test chance.'

Due to the constant rain, most of Australia's top-order batsmen were short of playing time as they prepared for their 11th scheduled first-class tour fixture against Warwickshire on a good wicket. An uncapped left-arm seam bowler, Stephen Rouse removed three of Australia's five wickets before lunch. Francis was trapped in front, shuffling uncomfortably across the crease. Ian Chappell chopped onto his stumps, and Watson stayed for an uneasy half an hour before he scored and then miscued a pull to midwicket. Greg Chappell's 17 briefly changed the mood of the innings, dispensing Rouse off the back foot, and Stackpole finally found some form, sweeping Peter Lewington for two to bring up his first 50 of the tour in 90 minutes. The celebration was short-lived when he fell to a catch by West Indian Lance Gibbs, when the ball looked like it was clearing the fence. Walters thumped Rouse through mid-on while Inverarity swung him to square leg to raise the half-century union. As Australia reached 330, Walters made 154 in just over even time, with one of his three sixes landing on the banks of the River Rea. Inverarity cobbled together 43. Walters had scored his second hundred in three days after waiting 42 innings in four years to hit his first in England, including a century in a session.

In a match filled with tension, Warwickshire's Mike Smith and West Indian left-hander Alvin Kallicharran played pivotal roles. Having just been informed of his return to England colours after six years, Smith faced a challenging start, playing and missing twice before being caught at first slip by Ian Chappell off Colley. Kallicharran stole the show, deflecting, cutting, and pulling his way to a commendable 62. Smith's undefeated second innings 78 further frustrated Australia's bid for victory, with the team needing another 108 in the final 20 overs.

After a fierce rainstorm swept the ground, Ian Chappell pondered the critical press. Chappell remained steadfast in his goal to win Test matches. He set media reports aside and redirected his thoughts to the main reason they were in England – to win back the Ashes.

New frontiers for cricket photographers

The year 1972 was the first time the regulations were relaxed to allow independent photographers into the grounds, a landmark change for cricket photography. Previously, only Sport and General, the photo agency, and Central Press had exclusive rights to Test matches in England. Outside English grounds it was common to see large screens erected to block the view. Such was the significance of allowing more photographers in that *The Times* celebrated the occasion by spreading John Edrich's dismissal for Surrey at Lord's across four of its front-page columns with a caption explaining the reason.

By 1972, Patrick Eagar, a Vietnam War photographer, former British standard tester, and now one of *The Cricketer's* magazine snappers, was coming into his own. Although restricted mainly to a position square of the wicket at Lord's, he found greater freedom to position himself at other grounds, creating a variety of perspectives on play.

Australian photographer Russell McPhedran was in England capturing images for the *Sydney Morning Herald* and the *Sun*. Making do with a small portable darkroom, he developed and printed pictures before transmitting them via a communications truck that accompanied the Australian tour – sending the photo via picture gram (like a fax machine) to reporters in Sydney. The Scotland-born McPhedran moved to Australia with his family in 1950, when he was 14. It wasn't long before he was working for Sydney's *Sun* newspaper, helping staff photographers at White City Stadium for the Davis Cup. Watching them snapping his tennis heroes was a dream come true. Using a Graflex camera, McPhedran learned the craft from senior photographers who stressed the need 'to have the story in your mind' before taking shots. This was long before automatic focus or motor drives, so photographers had to edit as they shot. Quick reflexes, and the ability to search for context in a scene while capturing the most essential elements, were essential. McPhedran later worked in Hong Kong, then Fleet Street at the *Daily Express*, covering the Profumo Affair and the Great Train Robbery in 1963. By late 1972, McPhedran was a senior photographer at Fairfax Media, where he was assigned to the Ashes tour. He packed his longest lens, a 400-millimetre, taking plenty of black-and-white film and a Nikon F2 camera.

One of McPhedran's favourite photos was of players and press sharing a meal during the Australian county match against Sussex, where everyone was wearing a tie bearing a donkey in pads. As revealed in his book *Stop the Presses: Russell McPhedran's Golden Years of Press Photography*, Dennis Lillee posed few threats to batsmen early in the tour. McPhedran would leave his post after half an hour to develop the photos and send them to Sydney to catch the last edition of the *Sydney Morning Herald*. Australia was bowling against Hampshire when he received a telex from head office thanking him but suggesting the pictures were boring and asking whether he could capture a shot of a wicket falling. McPhedran showed the telex to Ian Chappell, who passed on the message to Lillee.

'I'll see what I can do,' Lillee responded.

As McPhedran set up the following day, he heard English supporters discussing Hampshire opening batsman David Turner, who 'would surely play for England'. Turner had scored a fine 131 in Hampshire's first innings. McPhedran told them the batsman would be out inside the first hour. The photo the *Herald* received that day was of Turner looking forlornly back at his shattered stumps, bowled Lillee for 22. McPhedran thanked Dennis that night.

'No problem,' Lillee replied.

By the time of the First Test at Old Trafford, the Australians had played ten first-class matches, with three wins and seven draws, most of which were caused by inclement weather.

Chapter Four

First Test, Old Trafford

The timing of Manchester, the most northern venue, as the First Test host was an odd choice. Of the 20 Ashes Tests since 1884 at Old Trafford, there had been only eight results and 12 drawn matches, more than any other ground. As BBC broadcaster and writer John Arlott looked over a waterlogged and windswept ground, he provided a match preview for the BBC. 'In London, we have a raffle. The first prize is a week's holiday in Manchester, and the second prize is a fortnight in Manchester.' Continual rain had also denied the ground staff the chance to use the heavy roller on the match pitch.

The Australian selectors had much to ponder over who would play in the First Test. Despite his swashbuckling 176 against Hampshire, Graeme Watson had since struggled for runs. Ross Edwards was spending a lot of time in the nets during the two lead-in games, ruing missed opportunities mainly but impressing Richie Benaud, who wrote:

> It was heartening to see Edwards adjusting to the variable conditions ... he plays with bat and pad close together rather than playing across the batting line ... in direct contrast to some of the other Australians who are moving right across the crease and allowing the seam bowlers too much latitude.

There were, though, worrying signs for both sides. Bob Massie's ten-day injury, an abdominal strain, had yet to respond to treatment. England's quick Alan Ward, who dismissed Keith Stackpole and Ian

Chappell with successive deliveries for the MCC at Lord's, had a hamstring injury. Ward was injury-prone, having been flown back to England before the 1970/71 Tests with shin soreness and missing much of the 1971 home season after a blood vessel burst in his stomach.

The Australians had scrambled to find fashionable hairstyles before the First Test. Rod Marsh had been groomed by Lillee in the Australian dressing room after practice; Inverarity, Watson and Colley preferred an up-market salon in Manchester. Bruce Francis drove to Accrington for a trim by the hairdresser he used when playing in the Lancashire League.

When the Australians arrived at the ground on match eve, they found the practice wickets underwater, so they settled for a few laps of the oval, some exercises and a game of squash to warm up. It was a relief to be in tracksuits, away from the whites for a moment. Ray Steele delivered a message to the England camp via the press after he'd been asked about the threat John Snow presented to the Australian batting lineup. 'He took two for a hundred and plenty the last time I saw him bowl,' said Steele, typical of his bluster. He knew how to play psychological games with the opposition. Steele also knew Snow's dominance of Australia's top order in the previous Ashes series. It was true that Snow had been lacklustre when England played India and Pakistan at home the previous English summer.

Getting the mood right in a touring party before the First Test was always challenging. Ian Chappell adopted a low-key approach. Australia's match-eve dinner included a song written by Greg Chappell (containing lines about each team member) and sung by Paul Sheahan with Ross Edwards on guitar.

At first blush, the difference between the two sides was age. The average age of the Australians was 26.5 years; the English averaged 32. England's captain Ray Illingworth turned 40 on the first morning of the game while Mike Smith, on the verge of turning 39, returning after 47 Test appearances, had not appeared in England colours for six years. Norman Gifford was preferred to Derek Underwood, while the South African-born Tony Greig, at 25, was the youngster picked as an all-rounder. (Despite not having served the adequate qualifying time to represent England, the Australian Board of Control waived him through.)

Cartoonist Roy Ulyett in the *Daily Express* poked fun at the England selectors with a cartoon depicting Chairman of Selectors Alec Bedser on the phone to Ray Illingworth. 'Ray? Alec, here. I've just heard about WG; the doctor can't play at Manchester. Compton and Trueman are not available. Don't worry, we'll have to rely on youth. I'll get young "Dolly" and that kid Mike Smith with some spritely creeping between the wickets to liven things up. Enjoy your 40th birthday on Thursday, skipper. Remember, you're only young once.'

Jim Laker described the selections as 'unusual . . . sadly necessary and justified'. Illingworth was appointed England captain (initially for the first two Tests only). There were some good signs for England, Geoff Boycott had made a brilliant hundred in his final county match before the game and John Edrich had just hit a double ton against Kent. Stumper Alan Knott's two centuries in one match proved he was in form with the bat. D'Oliveira, despite being constrained by a hamstring injury, displayed power off the back foot in striking a brilliant undefeated 104 not out against Middlesex.

The three Australian newcomers to Test cricket, opener Bruce Francis, medium pacer David Colley and Ross Edwards, the eldest of the trio at 29, woke to a mixture of nerves and excitement. Edwards could scarcely believe his ears when the names of the Australian side were read out. 'I can still remember the scene in the Manchester dressing room the day before the Test when the twelve names were read aloud. I was holding a cup of tea in my hand when I immediately dropped it all over the floor.'

Colley, debuting because Massie was injured, looked at the dark clouds and thought it would be a good day for bowling, but he'd never been so cold. Francis wondered what John Snow might do with his pace and seam. Despite his nerves, Francis took comfort in the success he had experienced in two seasons with Essex. His 379 runs on tour revealed more consistency than any other batsman thus far. Edwards was soon told he was twelfth man, and knew his inclusion in the twelve was a sign that he couldn't be too far away from playing a Test.

Ray Steele reminded the press about Australia's aggressive approach: 'We are looking to win; draws are no good for us . . . our youth and enthusiasm could be vital.' Australia was full of potential. Watson, Inverarity, Greg Chappell, Marsh and Lillee had all played fewer than ten Tests. Worryingly, Greg Chappell had scored only one 50 in ten first-class outings, with a highest score of 83 not out against Nottinghamshire in early May.

Ian Chappell, whose 38 appearances placed him in veteran status in the side, was hoping to become the first Australian since Bill Woodfull in 1934 to regain the Ashes in England.

The *Sheffield Star*'s Basil Easterbrook observed, 'Until the Monday, those arriving at the ground reported they had not switched off the windscreen wipers of their cars until they were less than a mile away from Old Trafford.' The Manchester skyline, with over 30 church steeples and tall office blocks lit up, reminded observers how dark the summer sky was. In the days leading into the match, Old Trafford was the epicentre of a weather pattern that circled the Lancashire city for days, ensuring an absence of sun, warmth and light.

On the morning of the match, Adidas tracksuit-clad Australians limbered up with stretches and bicep curls. After a pitch inspection, umpires Charlie Elliott and Tom Spencer announced a 1 pm start. Due to niggling injuries and rain interruptions, John Snow had bowled just 36 first-class overs in ten weeks, taking only four wickets, and was struggling to remember the number of steps in his run-up. Players from both sides walked around the covered pitch as lawnmowers buzzed. The groundsmen were making the most of the break in the rain. Soon, a room attendant was ducking his head into the Australian change room, 'Mr Chappell, would you like to get changed with Mr Illingworth.' The Australian skipper looked at his teammates and replied, 'I know you're only doing your job, and I like Mr Illingworth, but I would like to get changed with my mates.' It seems extraordinary that almost a decade after the Gentlemen v Players divide was officially phased out, distinctions were still being made.

David Colley was so excited that he felt like running onto the field like football players did. On tour, Colley roomed with Lillee, and the pair found they had much in common. Colley was full of admiration for Lillee. 'I couldn't believe how tough, resilient and brave he was, and our job was to ensure that the English media wasn't aware that Dennis's back was troubling him.' Colley also learned from the hard work Lillee did away from the field. It would come in handy when Colley battled his own back problems as the tour progressed.

The crowd was minuscule amid swathes of empty blue seating for the opening morning. Piles of sawdust to help firm the bowlers' run ups sat untouched behind each set of stumps. Ray Illingworth won the toss while Ian Chappell looked at the hard pitch with grass on it, believing it wasn't a bad toss to lose. Chappell turned to the dressing room and rolled his shoulder slightly to let his teammates know they were in the field.

When Dennis Lillee, with splayed arms and wild hair, roared in from 40 metres, it was to four slips and a gully. England started shakily in murky conditions when Boycott survived an LBW appeal from the second ball of the match. The Australians' appeal reverberated around the stands, like the call of a newspaper seller entering a ghost town. Colley struggled through his first five overs, feeling nervous and cold, aiming to keep the ball pitched up.

Colley's 18th ball had Boycott edging hard, fast and low to Greg Chappell's left hand, but the chance went down. After 25 minutes, Edrich glanced his first boundary past Inverarity lurking at leg slip, before Boycott retired hurt after being hit above the left elbow by a short ball from Lillee. The arm struck was the same one McKenzie had broken in a one-day game in Australia less than 18 months before. Stackpole, standing at second slip, watched 'Boycott playing and missing at Lillee a dozen times in the first few overs'.

Lillee had Luckhurst lifting his hand off his bat handle when another ball sprung from a length. In a desperate attempt to run out Luckhurst, Lillee shied at the stumps before tumbling and rolling like an army officer at training drills before standing, smiling and rubbing the grass off his jumper. By lunch, 13 runs from seven overs had been scored.

Colley took his first wicket in his second spell when he knocked back Luckhurst's off stump with a yorker, the batsman craning his head back to watch the stump push back with neat precision. Until then, Colley had been wondering if he'd ever get a Test wicket. 'I thought I'll just have to hang in there, so I bowled a little off-cutter, not necessarily deliberately, and he [Luckhurst] missed it. It was a wonderful feeling.' Ian Chappell ran from first slip to offer a handshake as the Australians gathered around the New South Welshman. Watson ruffled Colley's hair as Marsh beamed a smile beneath his baggy green. When Gleeson almost bowled Edrich, Marsh and Chappell checked the stumps to check the ball hadn't gone through.

Lillee picked up Smith before Edrich, on 49, attempted a single to mid-wicket where one didn't exist and ended his three-hour stay.

With England sitting precariously at 3 for 99, the 200-centimetre-tall debutante Tony Greig, blond hair peeking out beneath his MCC cap, was dropped by Ian Chappell off Colley before he scored. Marsh cast a wry smile in his skipper's direction. Marsh had earlier fumbled a couple of balls only to be chastised by Chappell for his work with the gloves, 'C'mon, you're not out here for your good looks, you know. Start taking the bloody ball properly, will you?'

Greg Chappell's medium pacers removed D'Oliveira (using a bat with an image of his face on it), sending his off stump cartwheeling. Boycott returned to the crease adding only three before being lured forward by Gleeson and edging to Stackpole at slip. England lost half its wickets in four hours despite the butter-fingered Australians who caught only one of four catches offered. By stumps, and with England 5 for 147, the press had labelled the England side Dad's Army (a British TV sitcom about the UK's ragtag Home Guard during the Second World War).

The *Sun*'s Clive Taylor was more dramatic: 'England lay bleeding, victims after the first day . . . you needed nerve to watch it let alone play it.' There was no doubt the Australian bowlers, particularly Lillee, had harassed the English batsmen but Jack Fingleton wrote in *The Times*, 'The Australians had a too casual approach to their bowling rate as if they held the Ashes rather than England.' At times Lillee walked back to his 40-metre run up too slowly and bowled far too wide.

After play, England paceman Geoff Arnold, a draughtsman by trade, reset his mind by walking around the centre square. He examined Lillee's footsteps, amazed at the distance between them. 'I've got long legs, but if I took those sized steps, I'd get myself injured.' Arnold marvelled at the aggression Lillee showed and wondered whether England's batsmen were trying to play him too early for fear of being beaten for pace.

As the darkness deepened around the ground, Ian Chappell warmed himself next to a large heater, beer in hand in the Ladbrokes Marquee. He struck up a conversation with a young woman who had travelled from Melbourne to watch the series. He discovered she was a nurse who had cared for Graeme Watson at the Royal Melbourne Hospital the previous summer. As the two chatted, she revealed how Watson was given a tracheotomy and 'died' on the operating table before being brought back to life by the emergency teams.

Returning to his hotel room later that night Ian Chappell reflected on an exchange he had had with Marsh that day. When Chappell was persevering with bowling Gleeson and Inverarity, Marsh told his captain in blunt terms what he thought of the tactic. 'This is the greatest seamer's paradise of all time and you've got two spinners bowling . . . put some seamers – any seamers – on.' Chappell walked on but not before saying, 'I will remind you that one of those spinners just got Geoff Boycott out.' But Marsh was right. Chappell was captaining as if he was at Adelaide Oval, where the pitch was flatter and more conducive to spin.

Unsurprisingly, cold, blustery winds greeted the Australians warming up with an Australian Rules football at the start of day two while others slowly jogged around the ground. In his second over with the new ball, Colley trapped Greig low on the pads in front; his 57 on debut providing the backbone of the innings under challenging conditions. Knott fell ten runs later, having consumed 113 minutes for his 18. Illingworth appeared to edge behind but was given not out. Lillee, following through, stood next to the England captain, giving a mouthful. 'Get on your bike, you kangaroo,' Illingworth responded.

Colley took John Snow's off stump, tilting back like the leaning Tower of Pisa. Three wickets had fallen for 19 before Illingworth and Gifford added 34 in 75 minutes for the ninth wicket. The partnership ended when Gifford turned a ball from Inverarity to square leg, where Ian Chappell swooped and flicked it back to Marsh, who whipped the bails off. England's 249 was better than they had hoped for, adding 102 before their innings closed 80 minutes after lunch. Lillee's 2 for 40 from 29 overs was wayward at times, but Illingworth believed Lillee was two metres quicker than he was in the 1970/71 series. Gleeson bowled despite a hamstring strain, capturing 2 for 45 from 24.4 overs, but was rarely threatening. Colley's 3 for 83 off 33 overs proved successful in Massie's absence.

Just after half past three, Stackpole rolled his arms to keep warm as he walked out alongside the taller, lugubrious Bruce Francis. Shudders soon went through the Australian rooms when Stackpole edged

Arnold to Greig at second slip, who spilled the chance like a waiter losing control of his drinks. The next ball, Stackpole snicked finer to Snow, who dropped it while Francis scampered through for a single. Illingworth was starting to wonder how Snow had convinced him he would be an asset fielding in slips, but England was poorly equipped with close-in fielders. Francis then edged the next ball just short of Snow. The day two crowd of 12,000 moaned in despair, believing three chances in a row had gone down. Australia's openers recovered and put together the best first-wicket partnership against England in six years. The score was 68 by the time Bruce Francis was out lbw, playing back to a ball from D'Oliveira that hurried on. Stackpole believed the pitch, 'a seamer's paradise', was the most difficult he ever played on.

The longer Ian Chappell travelled in his international career the more mannerisms he picked up. He'd look at the sky on the way to the wicket, making sure his eyes were accustomed to the light. Once there, he'd constantly mark guard with the sprig of his right shoe, then play with his collar and clutch his box. Then, a shimmy of shoulders as he faced up. Jack Fingleton advised Chappell against fidgeting, especially with his box. Fingleton told Chappell how he had the same nervous impulse until some anonymous letters from spectators made him stop. At one point, Fingleton bought a baseball box from the US to try to rid himself of the habit.

When the crowd settled, Chappell faced Greig with a combination of twitches and defiance, hooking his first ball wide of off stump high and long to the deep fine-leg fence where Mike Smith leapt to catch. 'Good shot for fucking nowt, lad,' Illingworth said as he ran past Ian Chappell on his way to congratulate the bowler Tony Greig on his first Test wicket. Fingleton declared Smith's catch 'one of the most superb Test catches ever'. Watson lingered as the score stayed on 99 for 15 minutes before he hopped and edged Arnold to Knott for two. Australia went to stumps trailing England by 146 with six wickets in hand.

On day three Snow bowled successive maidens to an unusually becalmed Walters. When Greg Chappell pulled Arnold to the mid-wicket boundary it marked the first time Australia had reached the ropes for 27 minutes. Walters played and missed at three consecutive balls, then repeatedly flexed his left leg after being struck by late swinging deliveries from Arnold. Greig brilliantly caught Greg Chappell off Snow, diving to his left, holding the catch just above the ground at second slip. The tourists were scrambling at 5 for 119. Inverarity pushed forward to Arnold edging to Knott. Sir Leonard Hutton in the *Observer* rejoiced in the quality of England's attack. 'Any Australian batting side over the past 30 years would have been hard pushed to resist the magnificent bowling of Arnold and Snow.' With a first innings total of 142, Australia trailed 107 runs behind England. Snow's 4 for 41 revealed clever seam bowling rather than trying to blast the Australians out; Arnold took 4 for 62. Colley had marvelled at 'John Snow's ability to pinpoint a batsman's weakness and relentlessly pursue it'.

When England batted again, Boycott savagely hooked Lillee twice before, on 47, he was caught sweeping off Gleeson, who picked him up for the second time in the match. Gleeson had now taken Boycott's wicket six times in seven Tests. Luckhurst departed for a duck sparring at a lifting delivery from Colley, and D'Oliveira played and missed at the medium pace of Watson four times. At stumps on the third day England was 243 runs ahead with seven wickets in hand.

Slumped in the dressing room, David Colley noticed that despite the intimacy of the side-by-side rooms, Australians didn't mix with the England team after the day's play. 'They (England) just turned up, played, showered and off they went.' Mallett thought it was just part of the England way. 'They were so used to having to travel so much after a day's play I don't think it entered their minds to stay in the dressing room after play.' Press opinions on the game were now swayed. Ted Dexter wrote, 'Dad's army goes barmy . . . they suddenly looked like a Panzer division'.

At the start of the fourth day Ian Chappell continued to attack England, with D'Oliveira and Knott falling to Lillee. Smith grafted two-and-a-half hours for 34, at one stage failing to see a bouncer that whistled past his ears. Greg Chappell's medium pacers yorked Greig for 62, his second half-century of the match. Illingworth tried to leave a ball from Lillee, edged and was caught by Ian Chappell diving low to his right, a remarkable catch. While thunderous clouds rolled in, Lillee, with the new ball, took the last four wickets for none in six deliveries. His 6 for 66, including four wickets in six balls in England's second innings of 234, dispelled doubts about the Australian quick's fitness. Marsh finished the innings with five catches, equalling the record of England–Australia Tests shared by England's Jim Parks and Australia's Bert Oldfield, Gil Langley and Wally Grout (who performed the feat twice).

Ian Chappell was hopeful Australia, with 442 minutes and 20 overs to reach the imposing target of 342, could win. Only Bradman's 1948 Invincibles had overcome such a hurdle when they scored 3 for 404, winning at Headingley. When the Australian openers appeared under brooding skies, Francis fell lbw to Snow, stuck on the crease for six. Ian Chappell had scored seven before hooking and being given out caught behind, Knott gleefully pouching the ball before throwing it skywards. Chappell, grimacing, departed in his usual manner, tucking his bat under his arm and walking quickly toward the pavilion. With a day to play Australia was 2 for 57.

Bob Massie was now feeling fit enough to bowl half pace at Edwards in the nets. With the over-the-wicket area slightly elevated and wet, Massie bowled around the wicket (he had also bowled around the wicket when playing for Kilmarnock). Edwards, normally comfortable against medium pace, could barely lay bat on the ball. Massie remembered, 'Richie Benaud saw me bowling around the wicket to Ross and made something more of it than it was. Benaud spoke about it on the BBC highlights after the Old Trafford Test match.' Massie was just glad to bowl without pain.

By day five the pitch, taking on a darker hue, played slower. The outfield remained damp despite the day being sunny and cloudless and Australian wickets soon tumbled. Greg Chappell was caught at mid-on attempting to pull Arnold while Watson, changing his mind mid-stroke, played a tennis paddle, to be caught and bowled Snow. Jim Laker thought it the 'worst shot he'd ever seen from a Test batsman'. When Watson returned to the Australian dressing room he was greeted with silence. 'Chappelli didn't say anything; he didn't need to. I knew how bad it looked. I was terribly embarrassed by it. Devastated.' The stroke revealed Watson's uncertain state of mind. Despite the setback Watson maintained his intense desire to succeed. He had already given up his nightclub ventures in Perth with George Casellas to go on the tour. Watson knew he was now effectively a professional cricketer and had to succeed.

Stackpole advanced his overnight score from 28 to 67 before being bowled by Greig. The vice-captain's two half-centuries on a seaming pitch proved he was getting better at judging the line of the ball; learning when to leave and when to play at the ball. Walters batted uncertainly for 20 before playing on. Marsh, after a cautious start, struck Gifford deep into the crowd over long on, the first of his four sixes off the England spinner. It was selective hitting at its best. Joe Mercer, the former manager of Manchester City, sat with the Australians watching the Marsh onslaught and was quick to remind Chappell that his club also had a Rodney Marsh. When Marsh edged a wide delivery from Greig to Knott on 91, any chance Australia had of winning was lost. Marsh, though, had taken 'some pleasure in whacking him [Gifford] for four sixes', leaving the left-arm orthodox spinner with 0 for 29 from three six-ball overs. It was Marsh's second score in the 90s in Test cricket after he'd been left stranded on 92 when Lawry declared Australia's innings in the Melbourne Test in 1970/71. The defiant, lusty swinging helped Marsh and Gleeson add a valuable 104 in 82 minutes, giving Australia's total a look of respectability.

After losing 8 for 147 Australia finished with 252. By the time Gleeson, more agricultural in style than orthodox, departed for 30 Australia had lost by 89 runs. Gleeson's ability to stay at the crease was also an indication of how much the pitch improved. Snow had used his pace and guile to capture another four wickets, making it eight for the match. It had been 42 years since England won the First Test of a home Ashes series. Public interest was high, with 38,000 people attending across the five days despite the at-times arctic conditions. The Australians had at least gone down swinging. Marsh, in the second innings, had shown how the Australians could handle the England attack, marking a significant psychological shift after the battering of 1970/71. The AAP's Mike Coward thought when the Australians lost, they could have dropped their bundle but didn't largely due to Ian Chappell's 'steely resolve and an ability to keep his side thinking very positively'.

The Australian skipper continued to charm the press. When asked how he found the pitch, a smiling Ian Chappell scratched his head and answered, 'I wasn't there long enough to find out.' Even Chappell had to admit that being dismissed hooking in both innings for a total of seven runs wasn't a good look.

Not all Australians had taken the loss so well. *Daily Mail* columnist Paul Callan had gone to a London pub and ordered a gin and tonic minutes before closing time. He mildly taunted the Australian barman, who stared stonily back and announced, 'The bar is closed, mate.'

Ian Chappell had two problems leading into the Second Test at Lord's: Bob Massie's fitness and his own lack of Test runs. There were rays of light, the realisation that despite just two players reaching a half-century they had at times challenged England. Lillee had bowled pain free with pace, guile and a freedom of movement, while Colley proved he could be a useful backup bowler. Graeme Watson wasn't one to dwell on poor performances but he'd taken just one wicket in nine overs and managed two runs at Old Trafford.

Scores of just four and three had John Inverarity reflecting on his Test debut at the same ground in 1968, when he scored 34 in the second innings. Opening the batting with Bob Cowper on a beautifully paced pitch Inverarity likened it more to batting in club cricket for the University of Western Australia. Not so in 1972. 'The ball seamed around a lot, and it was very difficult batting. I remember Greg Chappell bowling his medium pacers to Basil D'Oliveira who played and missed at all six balls of the over.' In four innings, only 877 runs were scored, and there would have been fewer had the catching been better.

The English press was critical of Ian Chappell's hooking. Richie Benaud offered a staunch defence: 'Heavens, there has been some nonsense talked following the Old Trafford Test about the hook shot and the fact that Australia should never use it again on this tour . . . some of the finest strokes in the match were hook shots played by Stackpole and Marsh in the second innings. On the one hand, everyone screams for brighter cricket, and when the player gets out, he is immediately labelled irresponsible.' The Australians knew that to keep the series alive, they had to start winning, something they hadn't done since defeating India in Madras in 1969. Since then they'd lost seven of the 12 Tests they'd played. History was also against Ian Chappell. In the 20th century, only one Australian side losing the First Test had gone on to win the series (Bill Woodfull's team in 1930).

The next time the Australians gathered at the Waldorf Hotel Ray Steele held up a press report claiming they had taken the Old Trafford loss 'lying down', declaring, 'Pig's arse, we did.'

It didn't take long for criticism of the make-up of the Australian touring side to roll in. Western Australian-based journalist Kirwan Ward led the call for the return of Bill Lawry.

> He [Lawry] is the only known wicket-squatter who regularly beat my secret system for getting rid of stubborn batsmen who

> had been haunting the WACA wicket for too long. Sometimes I'll swear he was still out there at the crease, going through the batting motions in the dark, disregarding the fact that stumps had been drawn an hour or two before merely as a sneaky trick by the fielding side to get him out. But though Bill may be no Rod Marsh in the matter of having a go, the Australian team needs him now like a wheatbelt dam needs water.

Ward wasn't alone in his view. A proposal was put forward at a meeting of the Victorian Cricket Association that Lawry should join the Australian touring team in England, but it was defeated.

Ian Chappell's Australians also attracted attention for their fashion model looks. Long hair was in. So was facial hair. Perth's *Daily News* posed the important question, 'Who has the finest of them all?' with a photo below of the mustachioed Edwards, Lillee, Sheahan and Greg Chappell.

> Was it because of the bitter cold of the early English summer, was it the result of a bet or a date, or was it simply because wearing moustaches is the height of fashion in England? There is no telling the real reason for these four suddenly sprouting hairy growths on their upper lips . . . there's no question they will welcome the added protection against the cold, but who won the bet for the finest moustache? Is it Robert Redford (Edwards), Ringo Starr (Lillee), Pancho Villa (Sheahan) or Chappell (Harpo Marx)?

Just 20 hours after the end of the First Test the Australians travelled to Oxford to play Combined Universities. The big-hitting Pakistan opener and Universities' captain Majid Khan caused a giggle among the Australians when he arrived for the coin toss dressed like a Texas oilman, complete with Stetson hat. Bob Massie in his first outing for 25 days (having delivered only 356 balls so far on tour), bowled through the opening session. Coming around the wicket, he immediately reverted to a better line and length, removing Majid, caught behind.

Ian Chappell's frustration of playing weakened sides was on display. Dudley Owen-Thomas bent down to do up his shoelaces as Chappell walked past.

'I say, skipper,' he said, nodding at his bootlaces.

'Fuck off, pal. I only do up shoelaces for batsmen.'

Bruce Francis' double century, including one six and 32 boundaries in a five-and-a-half-hour stay, provided some much-needed confidence. Australia passed Universities' 277 with just two wickets down on their way to 8 declared for 478. Majid Khan provided the Australians with a lesson in sublime timing and hard-hitting, scoring 55 of the first 60 runs scored in the Universities' first innings (including three extras), and 85 in the second of a total of 202.

Losing the toss was becoming a habit for Ian Chappell when he called incorrectly for the eighth time in 11 matches against Essex at Ilford. West Indian import Keith Boyce then hammered 58 in the county's first innings of 238.

His first six scoring shots (4,4,4,3,6,3) helped Boyce reach 34 in just four overs. Ian Chappell opened, scoring 88 in a chanceless knock, while Greg Chappell's 181, his best score in England and only 16 short of his highest in all first-class cricket, dominated Australia's 9 declared for 435, their highest total on tour. Greg Chappell's driving was on full display, especially from mid-on to square leg, striking 29 boundaries and an effortless six in his 295-minute stay. As the tour progressed it was clear that Greg Chappell's stint playing for Somerset for consecutive summers (1968 and 1969) had given the South Australian a growing confidence in playing the moving ball off the seam.

When Australia bowled again, Bob Massie moved the ball considerably in the second innings, taking 2 for 34 from 13 overs, giving him four wickets for the match. Lord's now awaited.

Ross Edwards and Ashley Mallett were roommates made for each other on a long tour. Both were eccentric and well read, and they shared a similar sense of humour. The pair made a point of introducing themselves to all the guests at each function, no matter how boring or monotonous it proved to be. They also dressed up for breakfast each day. During the evening, they shared port and cigars in their room. Early in the tour, Edwards often asked Mallett to head down the street to the local off licence to pick up a bottle of port. When the habit was becoming expensive, Edwards wrote to the Australian Trade Commission at Australia House requesting supplies. In a matter of days, 144 bottles (12 cases) of high-quality Galway Pipe port were delivered to their room at the Waldorf Hotel. Edwards also penned a note to the Australian Wine Board with a promise 'to help promote the wines' when, as Australian players, they enjoyed local hospitality. Twenty crates of Australian wine duly arrived. By the mid-point of the tour, the Edwards/ Mallett room at the Waldorf was the most popular of all.

At Lord's the weather again turned bitterly cold as the three Australian selectors gathered at the edge of the centre square to discuss the possible line-up. Feeling the cold, Ian Chappell stood and folded his arms while Stackpole and Inverarity lay against the covers, half sitting up. By the end of the hour-long meeting, Bob Massie and Ross Edwards were in the side in place of Graeme Watson and John Inverarity. Dennis Lillee perambulated the centre square, examining the heavily grassed pitch. He smiled as he looked at Ian Chappell and Stackpole, saying facetiously, 'You blokes can't hook, can you?'

Lillee knew full well the pair's ability to hook and how the pitch's firm surface would lend itself to strokes square of the wicket. He was also aware of the debate in the press about whether Chappell should give the hook shot away, especially early in his innings.

Doug Walters noted the hardness of the pitch. He'd been hitting the ball well in the nets and had scored two successive centuries leading into the First Test. However doubt remained that Walters would ever crack the code of playing on English seaming pitches against high-quality seam bowling. It was seven years since his sparkling debut hundred against England at the Gabba but he had yet to find his feet at Test level in England. Expectations had been high when he boarded the plane with Bill Lawry's 1968 Australians (just days after his stint of national service) and early wagers laid in Sydney and Melbourne had him reaching 1000 runs by the end of May. It began with sponge-topped wickets and continual rain, as well as dual 80s in the opening Test at Old Trafford (81 and 86), but then faded with scores of 26 (albeit out of a team total of 78) 0, 46, 42, 56, 5 and 1. Walters' letdown could have been couched in terms of adjustment after a cricketer's convalescence following his national service, and becoming accustomed to the pace of the English wickets.

By 1972 the expectations were more real. Outside the Australians' inner sanctum, Walters had a reputation as laid back and laconic. His teammates knew him as the life of the party with a roguish sense of humour. He was the unofficial master of ceremonies on the tour coach and, in many ways, a born leader. Ian Chappell was confident the tide would turn for Walters, whom he considered a match winner. For England, Bob Taylor was excited at being on standby for Alan Knott, who had bruised his hand and needed to undergo a fitness test. The longest day of the year – midsummer – was on the Saturday of the Lord's Test. However, there were few signs the weather would improve.

Ian Chappell shared with his players the promise of television stations TVW7 (Perth) and SAS10 (Adelaide) offering the Australians a $10,000 incentive to regain the Ashes. Australian team manager Steele quickly dismissed the need for any incentive, 'because they are all keen to win'.

Chapter Five

Second Test, Lord's

In Lord's overcast conditions, the ball hooped late. Massie came around the wicket to the left-handers. Illingworth described it as 'rain without rain'. The atmosphere for the first three days at Lord's was heavy and humid, and the ball carried through with force to Marsh. Lillee and Massie bowled magnificently, and Colley delivered on his promise of genuine pace.

Massie's prodigious swing hadn't come as much of a surprise to Ian Chappell. He'd played against Massie in Shield cricket and watched his elevation to Australian ranks against the Rest of the World. Chappell remembered how Massie bowled Bill Lawry twice in one game. Not many bowlers did that. Chappell had also skippered Massie when he took seven wickets in an innings in the Rest of the World game in Sydney – his victims including Garry Sobers and Graeme Pollock. Massie would have played at Old Trafford but for injury, possibly the difference between the Australians winning and losing.

The Australians dined in a Piccadilly restaurant on the Lord's Test eve as part of the low-key lead in to the all-important match. Returning to the Waldorf, Stackpole and Francis walked along Aldwych in the chilled night air. Stackpole knew Francis was seen as Bill Lawry's replacement, an unenviable role.

Francis, a teetotaller and introspective, confessed, 'I don't know if I am good enough to play Test cricket.' Stackpole attempted to reassure him, but as the two entered the hotel doors, he wasn't sure his words had gotten through. Francis, shoulders slumped, returned to his hotel room, seemingly resigned to failure. Despite his 210 against Combined Universities just a week before, he lacked belief that he could translate first-class form to the Test arena.

Twenty-four-year-old Francis couldn't remember when cricket hadn't been part of his life. And here he was about to play in a Test match at Lord's. In contrast, Greg Chappell felt as comfortable as ever batting at an elite level, his mind focused having just come off 181 against Essex.

Even in the early 1970s, some of the Lord's crowd included gentlemen straight out of *Punch* – with their black suits, black bowlers, black briefcases, exiting black hearse-like taxis with *The Times* newspaper under their arms outside the WG Grace Gates. The sight of the green carpet of the perfect Lord's turf awaited, the weathervane Father Time motionless on top of the grandstand. Test greats like Keith Miller, Ray Lindwall, Denis Compton and Bill Edrich could have been spotted entering the ground. To the left was the cathedral-like Members' pavilion, its seats full of orange and yellow MCC ties. Flamboyant West Indian supporters entered the ground in large enough numbers to make their presence and support for Australia felt. For Caribbean cricket lovers, it was the start of an enormously successful decade for their side on English soil. Between 1948 and 1970, nearly half-a-million people had emigrated from the Caribbean to Britain, this large West Indian community often facing miserable living and working conditions, as well as racism and xenophobia. It was cricket, CLR James, the West Indian historian and Marxist writer observed, that provided comfort. Barracking for anyone but England became a major source of entertainment for Caribbean immigrants.

The players on the Pavilion balcony emerged as the public address system echoed around the Lord's ground. If rain interrupted play, there was always the museum at the back of the Pavilion to see Trumper's blazer, Hobbs' cap, Bradman's elf-like boots and a life-size portrait of Freddie Trueman. Despite being smaller in capacity than most Australian grounds, Lord's possessed considerable beauty, enhanced by the creation of the Harris Memorial Garden and the Coronation Garden behind the Pavilion. Lord's, with a membership of 16,000, was not considered just a cricket ground but a small estate with its ecosystem of groundsmen, caterers, electricians, museum attendants, painters, tennis professionals, typists and sales assistants who worked all year round.

Light rain fell. Ian Chappell and Ray Illingworth walked out of the Lord's Members' Pavilion and stood at the edge of the ground, but before they made it to the centre, heavier rain and poor light sent them back. Twenty-five minutes later, a growing crowd greeted the captains striding to the centre to examine what appeared to be a pallid, slow-paced pitch. Illingworth called successfully, signalling to his teammates that England would bat. Minutes later, umpires David Constant and Arthur Fagg appeared in the Australian dressing room with a box of a dozen balls. 'Would you like to pick a ball, captain?'

Massie looked on and asked, 'Can I pick the ball?'

'Mate, you gotta use it, go for your life,' Chappell replied.

Massie went through the box, carefully scrutinising each before selecting a darker one.

Alan Knott passed his fitness test in the England camp and Bob Taylor took twelfth-man duties. Geoff Arnold's ongoing hamstring tightness meant Middlesex opening bowler John Price was called into the side.

England reached 22 before Bob Massie, bowling into the wind from the Nursery End, hit Boycott's middle stump with a late in-swinging yorker. Marsh jumped for joy, knees to chest, while a buzz reverberated around the ground. Massie was relieved. 'I had at least one Test wicket.' Lillee, not yet at full pace, was gaining lift from the Lord's ridge. Luckhurst was beaten for pace, caught on the front crease, as the ball tipped the off-stump bail. When Edrich was lbw to Lillee, three wickets had fallen for six runs in 15 minutes before England steadied. D'Oliveira struck successive boundaries off Lillee – a magnificent hook ahead of square leg and a fierce drive in front of point to take England to 66. Ian Chappell walked to Massie and held him gently by the shoulders.

'I'm stuffed,' Massie said.

'You're still bowling well,' said Chappell, 'you've got to keep going.'

Chappell's encouragement worked. Massie reverted to bowling over the wicket (after most of his lengthy spell around), trapping D'Oliveria in front with the last ball of his 16th over. Greig took 20 minutes to get off the mark while Smith kept chancing his arm playing across the line of the ball. When Massie bowled him with a dipping yorker, he had bowled unchanged for 20 overs, taking 3 for 43 as England staggered to 5 for 97. Francis dropped a sitter off Knott just in front of square leg when the England keeper mistimed a pull shot.

Knott and Greig enjoyed a partnership of 96 before Knott was out for 43, trying to steer Massie through the slips and edging to Colley in the gully. Within minutes Greig nicked Massie to Marsh after scoring his third 50 in three innings.

England was 7 for 249 by stumps, with Illingworth undefeated on 23 and Snow on 28. After play, the England side studied a film of Massie's bowling action, but it was transposed showing the swing bowler delivering left-handed and John Edrich batting right-handed. The players decided to head off to the pub, 'where they should have gone in the first place', Mallett later dryly observed.

As Friday morning dawned, crowds lined up to enter Lord's. On request from the Australian captain, twelfth man Jeff Hammond peppered Ian Chappell with bouncers in the nets. 'Even your mates are trying to bounce you out,' a fan quipped. Chappell was still undecided whether to keep hooking or not. Ken Barrington visited the Australian dressing room and advised Ian Chappell not to hook until he'd reached 50. Just after 11 am, 29,000 crammed into Lord's to watch Massie take five overs to strike with the second new ball. First, Illingworth was lbw caught in front with a ball that nipped back off a good length. Then Snow was bowled, and Norman Gifford edged to Marsh, giving Massie his third wicket of the morning from 31 balls while conceding just nine runs. With the sun only occasionally breaking through the clouds, England was all out for 272 as Massie walked from the ground surrounded by teammates.

Massie's figures of 8 for 84 on debut had the statisticians reaching for the record books. Only one other Australian, Albert Trott, had taken 8 for 43, in a game against England in Adelaide (in the second innings) of his first match in 1895. Massie was the fifth Australian to capture eight or more wickets in an innings against England. Ironically, the last Australian to do so was Graham McKenzie, with 8 for 71 in a Test against the West Indies in 1968/69. For Massie, it was a dream come true. 'Every time we played cricket as kids in the backyard, we would imagine we were playing at Lord's. I couldn't believe I had taken eight wickets.' Since he boarded the plane to England, Massie had plotted how to remove England's top order. 'I knew that to John Edrich, I had to go around the wicket. Edrich left the ball so well that I went around the wicket to move the ball into him . . . I was going to go back over the wicket but thought I'd wait for a bit.' Western Australian teammate Ian Brayshaw wasn't surprised at Massie's ability to loop the ball in late. 'Massie, at his best, was unplayable. Fielding at second slip at the WACA, I could almost count the row of stitches on the ball. He had great wrist flexion, and his right-hand fingers were almost touching his forearm in the load-up. Massie's wrist flexion was able to put underspin on the ball.'

Ray Illingworth didn't think anyone could have played Massie in the conditions, but he also credits Dennis Lillee. 'Dennis was bowling up the slope from the Pavilion End, and no one could get a touch on him.'

The sun was out when Australia batted and slumped to 2 for 7. Francis, caught on the crease, was beaten for pace and bowled first ball by Snow. Stackpole was late on the hook and caught by Gifford at forward square leg off Price. Still unsure about hooking, Ian Chappell was hit by short balls from Snow. Chappell then decided he would assert himself, and hooking the short ball was critical.

The Chappell brothers added 75 as England's bowlers tried to contain them. Greg Chappell was becalmed on 14 for close to an hour. He remembered it as a moment of realisation about focus; to block out the externals and watch the ball.

> I can't recall concentrating harder, not being forced to concentrate. We were in deep trouble and somehow had to get somewhere near England's 272. I was so determined not to give my wicket away that I went for what must have been my longest time in Test cricket without hitting a boundary. I reckon my first one came after three hours at the crease.

His brother moved more aggressively, reaching 50 in 122 minutes before hooking a ball from Snow into the Mound Stand. His innings ended six runs later, hooking Snow to long leg, where Mike Smith caught the ball just above the ground. Walters poked at Snow and was caught by Illingworth in the finer of the two gullies for one. Greg Chappell continued driving through the arc from mid-wicket to cover, charging closer to three figures as he exquisitely glanced Snow to the boundary and drove Price to the extra cover boundary off the front foot.

Ross Edwards, on debut, revealed a technique ready-made for Test cricket before pulling Illingworth to Smith, who took the running catch at deep square leg. The grey-haired Smith, referred to as 'Steptoe' from the TV show *Steptoe and Son* by the Australians, continued to surprise with his athleticism (he had been an excellent close fielder when he captained England in 1965/66). In poor light, Gleeson was sent in as a nightwatchman and helped scamper the five runs that took Greg Chappell to his century before stumps.

The suspicion that Greg Chappell's batting leaned too heavily to the on side was dispelled when he maintained his ability to whip the ball off his toes and hip. David Frith observed his style as

> tall, with an upright almost Edwardian stance, he makes when he drives a characteristically strong commitment to the front foot; the body bends forward over the fulcrum of the braced left leg, giving him such a commanding airborne view of the oncoming ball that it is the plainest formality that should be dispatched with power and certainty . . . And the manner his right foot kicks up high behind the stroke is nothing less than arrogant.

Born a week before Bradman's last Test match, Greg Chappell was now one of the significant differences between the sides. John Arlott identified 'only two timing errors, a sweep that did not connect and a belated cut'. Chappell's masterclass of 131 finished after six hours and 12 minutes when he played on to D'Oliveira. Chappell threw his head back in surprise before departing before a standing ovation from the packed MCC Members.

Ian Chappell thought the knock was equal to Massie's eight first-inning wickets. Decades later, Keith Stackpole watched the match again on television and realised the greatness of Greg's knock. 'Watching from an excited and nervous dressing room, it was hard to appreciate how good Greg's innings was.' The man himself still rates it as the best innings he played.

> I only made one mistake, and that was when I got out. To bat that long and not make a mental mistake was the greatest achievement of my batting career; I was so attuned mentally and didn't make any physical mistakes either . . . It was a wicket for the bowlers, and the ball was doing quite a bit.

Rod Marsh's contributions with the bat were more like a middle-order batsman. His boisterous half-century in 72 minutes ended when he edged Snow to Greig at second slip. Massie's bowling heroics weren't extended to the bat when he was caught by Knott off Snow for a duck. Australia was bowled out for 308 half an hour after lunch on the third day.

Ian Chappell gathered his players in a huddle. 'All I want is a wicket or two before they pass our total.' England was 36 runs behind on the first innings. Lillee reminded Massie that it was 'our responsibility to knock off one of these openers'. It took just one hour to break the back of England's batting. Boycott, on six, went back and was struck high on the thigh pad, only to watch as the ball fell on top of his stumps. Lillee danced down the wicket, eventually falling into Marsh's arms. Boycott spent the next half-hour circling the big table in the Lord's dressing room. 'Blerdy Colley slogs for 25, and I'm out playing properly for six. There's no blerdy justice in this game.' Marsh happily took Luckhurst's tentative hopping prod as England fell to 2 for 12. Edrich edged Massie to Marsh, who kangaroo-hopped to celebrate, before D'Oliveira snicked to Greg Chappell taking the catch low down at third slip. By tea England were 4 for 29 with Lillee and Massie bowling unchanged.

As Lillee took his first spell, Ian Chappell approached Colley and said, 'I'd like to see your express pace right now.' Immediately, Colley defeated Greig with a ball that dipped back sharply from outside the off stump. Colley hit Smith above the pad, but umpire Fagg ignored two full-blooded appeals. Colley conceding just eight runs from seven blistering overs was crucial to Massie's swinging wicket-taking show at the other end. Colley remembered it as the best he had ever bowled.

'You have days when you bowl poorly and get six wickets. I wish the wickets had come that day at Lord's.' Colley was so quick that Marsh stepped a metre forward when Lillee came on to bowl. Ian Chappell thought the spell vital. 'I reckon that [Colley's spell] was the straw that broke the camel's back. Smith had already been hit by Dennis all over the body after Lillee had done everything he could to get him out. It was almost as if it was all too much for Smith.' By tea, England was five down. Stackpole looked on from the slips wondering why the English batsmen were snicking to everyone but him. Walters fielding in the gully baited his vice-captain, 'It's a Tommy Hanlon. It's a Tommy Hanlon.' Stackpole wondered what Walters was on about until he caught Illingworth off Massie. 'There you go, you bugger,' Walters said, slapping Stackpole's back. He finally twigged. Tommy Hanlon hosted a TV quiz show, *It Could Be You*. Stackpole just laughed. By stumps, England was 9 for 86, and Massie had seven.

Given the game's pace, the MCC officials were worried about an early finish, but a 25-pence increase on the outer gate meant receipts reached £81,500, a record for any England Test match. It was enough for John Woodcock to describe the public interest in the game as 'like old times to hear that they were queuing at Lord's at four o'clock on the Saturday morning and closing the gates soon after 11'. The louder Australian fans recreated the Sydney Cricket Ground's Hill in front of the Tavern at the Pavilion End, using the repetitive chants of English soccer fans to urge on Lillee and Massie. Ian Chappell thought the crowd was the best he had played in front of, although there was some beer throwing. Some fans from the 'Australian quarter' also ran onto the ground when Greg Chappell brought up his century. Some of the diehard MCC Members bristled at the behaviour. It rankled almost as much as the new advertising hoardings and betting marquees at Lord's. After play on Saturday (before the Sunday rest day), Daphne Benaud, acting as Ray Steele's assistant, contacted Massie to see if he could attend Madame Tussauds for a press shoot of him standing next to a wax figure of Garry Sobers the next day. Once there, Massie was asked by the press to go to Lord's so they could capture images of him bowling. Massie changed into his whites but deliberately muddled his action when he bowled in the nets. Later that day, when Massie told Stackpole, the Australian vice-captain chuckled to himself. Stackpole knew he could read Massie's action by watching on from second slip. On Monday before play, the

England selectors announced Ray Illingworth as captain for the final three matches. Tailender John Price, encouraged by an offer of a pound per run toward his benefit fund, defiantly added 35 in 48 minutes with Norman Gifford before England was sent packing for 116.

Massie, in a short-sleeved jumper leaping almost vertically with two hands raised, features in a photo by Patrick Eagar. His snap, taken on the fourth day, captures Massie's triumph (16 wickets for 137). As the Australians walked off the field, Ian Chappell made sure his players stood back to allow the modest, side-burned debutante to go through. Only two bowlers, Jim Laker (19) and Sydney Barnes (17), had taken more wickets in a Test. By the time Australia batted, the sun was out again as Bruce Francis, on a pair, trudged out with Stackpole to help chase 81 to win. Soon enough, Francis again found himself entombed at the crease, caught behind Price for nine. Stackpole struck three successive boundaries off Tony Greig; a front-foot drive through the covers, a back-foot drive, and a glide past D'Oliviera at third slip. Australia wobbled before going to lunch when Ian Chappell edged to Luckhurst at slip off D'Oliviera but, after the break, Stackpole attacked the bowling to be undefeated on 57. The winning runs were scored in 104 minutes.

The Australians wasted no time whooping it up in the dressing room, celebrating their first win under Ian Chappell. Team masseur Dave McErlane tap-danced through the Lord's dressing room to join the festivities. Hundreds of fans waited outside while a number managed to climb into the Australian dressing room.

A shirtless Massie in a long-sleeved jumper made impersonations of John Arlott and comedians Peter Cook and Dudley Moore, as congratulatory telegrams came in from around the world. As Stackpole watched John Snow shaking hands and offering congratulations to Australia's new swing king, he couldn't help but feel sympathy for Massie. Stackpole knew the weight of expectation that now sat heavily on his teammate. 'Cricketers only get a certain amount of luck in their careers. I wondered if Bob used all his luck up in one Test match.' While admiring Massie's ability to bowl unchanged through the second innings, Ian Chappell thought a fairer spread of wickets would have been Massie 10, Lillee 8 and Colley 2. 'Ferg [Massie] bowled bloody well, and we caught everything they nicked. Dennis bowled bloody well, and getting Boycott out in the second innings was crucial.'

After Massie's blitz of the England batsmen, headlines rang with lines such as, 'Massie went thataway or was it thisaway?' (*Daily Express*), 'Mauler Massie Wreck England' (*Daily Mirror*), and 'So near a Massiecre' (*Sun*). He was dubbed 'the new maestro of swing'. While much of the talk was about Massie's success, Trevor Bailey in the *Financial Times* observed, 'The outcome was that they were so pleased to get to the other end [from Lillee] and face the more gentle pace of Massie that they understandably relaxed, which proved fatal.' Richie Benaud saw Massie's performance as 'technically one of the best pieces of swing bowling I have had the pleasure of watching . . . Massie and Lillee are the most exciting combination since Miller and Lindwall were at their peak'.

The cumulative crowd of 82,441 spectators was reported to have paid the highest cash receipts for any cricket match. Not bad for three-and-a-half days. Sadashiv Palsule from India's multi-language press service questioned the claim. On notepaper headed 'The Multi-Language Press Service of India with offices in Bombay, Delhi, Poona, Ahmedabad and 9 Beechcroft Avenue London, N.W. 11' Palsule stated he believed the record belonged to India, where takings exceeded £100,000 in Test matches against Australia at Madras, Bombay and Calcutta two years earlier. Whatever the truth, the high match attendance must have continued to stoke the growing revolutionary fire within Ian Chappell regarding player payments.

A more immediate question concerned royalty. Having finished before the traditional Queen's visit at tea on the fourth day, the match presented cricket authorities with a dilemma. Amid the champagne-soaked celebrations, Ray Steele told Ian Chappell, 'We've got a problem.'

'What's the problem?' the Australian captain replied. 'We've just won a Test match.'

'We've been asked to meet the Queen at Buckingham Palace for afternoon tea at 5 pm.'

The crowd outside the Grace Gates applauded as the Australians in Executive Ford cars drove out in a convoy to Buckingham Palace to meet the Queen. When they arrived at the gates of Buckingham Palace, Mallett and Sheahan wound down the windows and shouted in celebration. As the cars approached the gravel, Lillee screeched his car to a stop. A well-dressed man resembling the choirmaster in the *Vicar of Dibley* greeted the Australians flamboyantly. 'Oh, you must be the Australians, oh do come in.' Despite the various states of sobriety, the visit to meet the Queen was carried off with minimal fuss.

The English press was frustrated by the lack of access to the Australian players. After the Lord's Test, Massie, like all his teammates, bar the captain, was banned from speaking to the media. Only the captain could talk to the press. The ban had been in place since 1965 after Norm O'Neill had told the media in the West Indies that chucker Charlie Griffith 'would kill somebody one day'. The main comment came from manager Steele, who said,

> I can only describe it [Massie's bowling] as a Laker-like performance. I have never seen such a magnificent performance in cricket before . . . He came in and just flaked out on a chair with his feet up and drank a couple of bottles of lager straight off.

There was little doubt that England's top order was struggling, as John Woodcock reported after Lord's in *The Cricketer*. John Edrich's last 15 innings had produced only 358 runs. Brian Luckhurst's last 12 amounted to 263 runs, and Geoff Boycott's last seven produced 121 runs.

The *West Australian*'s cartoonist Allan Langoulant depicted a

'Do not disturb' sign hanging from a brass doorknob of room 437 [Massie's] at the Waldorf Hotel. Reporters descended on his parent's Bedford home in Perth as congratulatory phone calls rolled in. Former Western Australian cricketer turned journalist Keith Slater fought his way through the champagne corks. 'The telephone never stopped ringing for the whole hour, and the Massies worked a roster system answering it.' Massie's father Arnold, a chiropodist and a Scot born on a lighthouse in the North Sea, recalled his son's 'initial preference was for spin', inspired by watching Arnold bowl in the family backyard. He put any movement down to the ball hitting a twig. 'Funny how it hits the same twig all the time,' grinned the young Bob, whose interest in making a cricket ball 'do tricks' grew (and modified to include swing). When Slater fired the questions, Arnold pointed to the chair Bob sat in after each match. 'He would sit there, put his feet up and open a bottle of beer, shut his eyes and sing, "All I have to do is dream, dream, dream"' – before Arnold added, 'If a Scot sets his mind to do something it will be done.'

Later that day, Massie's Scottish wife Nancy was the centre of attention after being photographed at work in long white lace-up boots, a mini-skirt, long-sleeved top and large wrist bangles. Nancy's eye-catching attire was perfect for the narrative, depicting the glamorous wife keeping the home fires burning while her husband was away playing for his country.

After the embarrassing loss at Lord's, the English press revealed a capacity for honesty and snobbery. The *Daily Mail* featured an 'anonymous correspondent' eavesdropping on the reaction from the Members. The scene involved two well-dressed men of 'impeccable lineage' speaking to each other.

'Ah yes, Thomas, but it was awfully good cricket.'

'Awfully good cricket be damned. We weren't merely beaten. We were rooted.' The correspondent noted, 'If that word is new to you, it is an Australian expression which is neither bespoke nor impeccable.

It simply expressed what Australia did to us. We were rooted out of sight, which is what tends to happen if you give an Australian an inch or an encouraging nod or patronising smile.'

Perth's *Daily News* immediately launched a special fund to pay tribute to Massie's 16-wicket haul. Within 24 hours, it had reached $1000.

The day after the Lord's Test, the Australians attended the National Sporting Club Dinner at the Café Royal, London. Guest speakers were MP Clement Freud, grandson of Sigmund Freud, celebrity chef and writer, and BBC broadcaster John Arlott. As the players settled for their meals, Doug Walters sat beside the imposing Freud and placed a packet of cigarettes on the dinner table.

'I hope you don't intend to smoke any of those,' came the booming response from Freud. Walters hurried off to inform his teammates he was seated next to 'a right pommy bastard who was allergic to smoke'. After the speeches and knowing Freud had to give the closing toast, Paul Sheahan and Walters smoked cigars and deliberately blew smoke into his face. Mallett remembers Freud falling backwards into the curtains off the stage, much to the delight of the Australians.

The night ended up being a long one. They left the National Sporting Club Dinner at midnight and headed to a Marble Arch recording studio to record songs 'Here come the Aussies' and 'Bowl a ball, Swing a bat', written by English pop singer Daniel Boone and professional songwriter Rod McQueen. *Here come the Aussies* begins

> Here comes the Aussies and cricket is the game.
> We're all together, and winning is our aim.
> We'll play on through the English rain and win the Ashes back again . . .

To the musical purists, sadly, it doesn't get much better.

The recordings had involved significant planning. The Australians had left the dinner dressed in dinner jackets, dark glasses and smoking cigars, and the Penny Farthing record label supplied cases of beer to help the Aussies loosen up, although it's fair to say they were probably well on the way. Some sat on chairs, others stood, three or four to a microphone. The two songs took four hours to record, marking the first time an Australian cricket team had made a record since the Donald Bradman chorus more than 30 years earlier. 'Here Come the Aussies', the A side on *Chappell's Aussies*, was belted out to the tune of the Chelsea Football Club song 'Blue is the Colour', released when they played in the League Cup final in 1972 and also issued by the Penny Farthing Record label.

Colley remembered,

> We turned up in all kinds of disarray . . . one or two of us were inebriated by the time we arrived. Ian Chappell wanted to get away as quickly as possible for reasons he didn't share with us, so he got the shits when we all started mucking up and singing in strange ways. The technical crew in the studio were beside themselves and didn't know what was happening. It was typical of aspects of the tour. When we weren't knuckling down (to play), we had a lot of fun.

Sheahan described the recordings as a 'triumph of the sound engineers'.

On 30 June, the *Sun* featured Ian Chappell's Australians dressed in 'true Frank Sinatra style' in a double-page spread under the headline 'Aussies sing songs for swinging sixties'. Ian Chappell holds a beer between takes, and his brother Greg, in Johnny Ray style, has his right hand to his ear. The royalties were expected to exceed $1500. The reality was underwhelming. There were 10,000 copies distributed in England and the same number air freighted to Australia. Perhaps unsurprisingly, 'Here Come the Aussies', with B side 'Bowl a Ball, Swing a Bat', briefly proved a number one hit in Perth's small market.

The record's local success was helped by the newly appointed music director of 6PR, 22-year-old Cherie Edwards (Ross's cousin), who gave the songs plenty of airtime. Cherie was the first female music director in Australia and was profiled in Perth's *Daily News* with a sizable photo spread wearing a mini skirt, high black boots and a long-sleeved shirt, holding the single, sitting on a radio panel next to a turntable. 'I think it is a typical Australian singalong,' she is quoted as saying, 'which could be a hit given one ounce of luck.'

Chapter Six

The road to Trent Bridge

As on all tours the players' memories of touring England in 1972 centred on experiences rather than on-field performances. The Australian squad was in high demand to appear at various functions, some of which were more memorable than others. One night, ten of the Australian touring party attended a play featuring actress and model Joanna Lumley. After the performance of *Don't Just Lie There Say Something*, the Australians were asked backstage to mix with the staff and join them for a midnight dinner. A bikini-clad Lumley appeared holding a cricket bat as light bulbs flashed, capturing the Australians enthusiastically looking on. Bruce Francis recalled another fascinating evening seated next to Formula 1 motor racing legend Graham Hill, who died three years later in a plane crash.

Social distractions were good for Francis, who wrote to his girlfriend Shelley every day, eventually spending all his tour money calling her from Australia. Australian journalist Phil Wilkins even penned a postcard to Bruce's father Cass with the message: 'We need to get Shelley to England. Bruce will play better.' Francis could at least laugh at himself. After his first-ball duck at Lord's, he went out with friends and ordered duck for dinner.

The tour provided plenty of opportunities for private sightseeing. After the Lord's Test, Ian Chappell and Rod Marsh stayed in London for an eight-day break, where they played golf at Denham, Wentworth West (one of the most challenging courses in England),

and Sunningdale. Marsh described in his autobiography *You'll Keep,* how the Australian captain helped cement their relationship.

> On each of those days, Ian and I played golf. We would sleep till about 11 o'clock, miss breakfast and go straight to the golf club, where we had lunch. Then we'd hit off, play a round, have a few drinks at the clubhouse and a slice of the London nightlife before flaking out in bed for another long sleep. That was our routine for a blissful eight days.

When they joined Ted Dexter for a round at Sunningdale, Ian Chappell and Rod Marsh looked on in admiration as Dexter shot 32 for the front nine. Chappell scuttled his drive at the tenth hole. His caddy looked up and commented, 'Aye, that's the way, laddie. If you're goin' to fook 'em up, fook 'em up straight.'

Meanwhile, the Australians lost a 50-over game against the Cricketer's Association in Nottingham. The loss was Australia's third on tour and second in a minor one-day fixture. As the Australians bussed the 225 kilometres to the historical city of Bath on the banks of the River Avon, the mood was one of optimism as players caught up on sleep, read and wrote letters home.

When the Australians played Somerset, they relied on inside knowledge of the Bath ground from Greg Chappell, who had passed the 1000-run mark for Somerset there in 1968. Kerry O'Keeffe, playing for Somerset in 1972, provided a familiar Australian face. A reminder of the dominance of veterans on the county circuit was 41-year-old Somerset captain Brian Close.

Somerset reached 6 for 131 before the players again scampered off in heavy rain. When the Australians batted, Watson (32), Sheahan (30), and Inverarity (0) did little to further their Test claims. O'Keeffe was disappointing. He bowled with an even flatter trajectory than in Australia, and took just one wicket from eight featureless overs. In contrast, Ashley Mallett's 5 for 59 placed him in the frame for a Test recall. Close declared while acting Australian skipper Stackpole's late order 57 gave Australia the edge before the heavens opened up again, and the match was called off.

Australia was now scheduled to play Leicestershire. The county, led by Illingworth, was no easy beat. It had won two one-day competitions and placed second in the County Championship. The controversially discarded Australian Graham McKenzie had also just taken his second hat trick for the county that summer. As the team bus arrived at the Grace Road ground, McKenzie, the three-time England tourist, was one of the first to greet them.

Ian Chappell noticed his old teammate looking even more 'like an Adonis'. He was bowling like one, too, having taken 40 wickets that season (his third for Leicester). After fielding practice, Chappell and McKenzie, on the Australian change room balcony, discussed the England players' strengths and weaknesses. Chappell admitted he was grappling with the form of opening batsman Francis, who had struggled to make a start in three of his four Test innings. Francis' form did not improve. He made just 16 before one of Peter Stringer's medium-pacers snuck through his defence. Paul Sheahan motored to his first ton in first-class cricket since 1969, finishing with an undefeated 135. Significantly, Lillee and Massie routed Illingworth's Leicester side for 58 in just 24.3 overs. Massie's 6 for 30 and Lillee's 3 for 25 reminded the England selectors of the potency of their combination.

There was humour for both sides when Australia bowled again. Having pocketed a young boy's tennis ball from the boundary, Lillee used it to bowl a bouncer at McKenzie that flew high over a shocked McKenzie's head. Initially, he thought Lillee had transgressed the fast bowlers' agreement to not bowl bouncers at each other but laughed when he realised Lillee had bowled a tennis ball. By stumps on the second day, the Australians had taken 16 wickets for 249, and Leicester had fallen to 6 for 191 in its second innings. Massie's 4 for 9 from 28 balls made short work of the tail as Australia cruised to a win by an innings and 46 runs. Massie's tour tally of wickets had risen to 41 at 12.63.

England's 'Dad's Army' tag was starting to ring true. The AAP mocked the selectors' approach, featuring a headline, 'Another Hope for England?' The article showcased an 84-year-old village cricketer named John Cobbald. Cobbald, a one-time Surrey county player, remembered watching W.G. Grace bat and still opened the batting for Old Ipswichians' second eleven.

Undaunted, Alec Bedser, Cyril Washbrook and Alan Smith continued their approach by picking a squad of 13 for the Third Test that included batsmen Peter Parfitt and John Hampshire, all-rounder Richard Hutton, and pace bowler Peter Lever. Parfitt, at 35, was considered strong against the quicks and a renowned slips fieldsman. He had toured Australia in 1962/63 and 1965/66 and played the West Indies in 1969. Hutton (son of Sir Leonard), at 29, was considered one of 'the up and comers', having already played five Tests against India and Pakistan. The Australians believed he posed little threat with the ball, having taken just 3 for 181 for the Rest of the World against Australia in 1971/72. Hampshire at least had a debut Test century against the West Indies to his name. While good on paper, Lever had struggled with a back injury that prevented him from playing for Lancashire against Australia at Manchester in May. Boycott was unavailable after being struck by a bouncer from Bob Willis, the injury requiring ten stitches in the middle finger of Boycott's right hand. Brian Luckhurst, with innings of 14, 0, 1 and 4 in the first two Tests, was lucky to be retained, although he had decent county form, scoring an undefeated 184 and 63 against Surrey, as well as 73 and 98 not out against Middlesex.

With the need to balance team form with the conditions, Ian Chappell and his co-selectors were at odds over who should play in the Third Test at Nottingham. The ambition of frustrated players on a long tour also had to be managed. Even harder was when one of the frustrated players was a co-selector, as with John Inverarity. Chappell doubted Inverarity's ability as a Test-class batsman but recognised that he could be a useful left-arm-orthodox bowler in the right conditions. Chappell was aware Inverarity wanted to open the batting to secure a Test spot. Preparing for the clash against Middlesex at Lord's, Stackpole had told Chappell that Inverarity was 'going to put his hand up to open the batting'. When Inverarity raised the matter at the selectors meeting, Stackpole's blunt response made it clear that Inverarity would not be opening the batting in the Tests. Having just scored 54 against Leicester at the top of the order, Inverarity's claims had merit. Inverarity had also opened for Australia in the first and last two Test matches of the 1968 Ashes, including scoring a defiant 56 in Australia's ill-fated second innings on a damp pitch at The Oval. There was no doubt Francis' position was vulnerable. He'd scored 27, 6, 0 and 9 at Old Trafford and Lord's and dropped his last six catches in the field, including three in Tests.

Despite his misgivings, Ian Chappell allowed Inverarity to open against Middlesex at Lord's but, as if on cue, rain washed out the first day's play. Only three of 17 tour matches were so far unaffected. When play did begin at Lord's, Parfitt's aggressive 68 enabled future England captain Mike Brearley to declare at 2 for 192. Inverarity was bowled by Price for a duck in his only innings, while Australia declared overnight at 3 for 167, made at a run a minute. Marsh had a rare rest with a slightly bruised hand, giving reserve keeper Brian Taber an appearance at Lord's and a reward for his patience and support to Marsh.

Despite the enormous interest in the series, ticket sales were poor in the days leading to the Third Test. Acting secretary at Trent Bridge, Tony Saunders, privately wondered why only £6500 had been spent on tickets. Saunders needn't have worried. A record gate receipt of £41,748 would soon be made.

Chapter Seven

Third Test, Trent Bridge

As Keith Stackpole tucked his bat and pads under his arms and headed back to the Nottingham dressing room after practice, journalist Phil Tresidder told him, 'I'm betting on you to score a hundred.' With marquees at every ground, gambling was easily accessible. (Trent Bridge was the first of the counties to introduce a betting office for cricket and horse racing.) Tresidder's comment stuck in Stackpole's mind, along with the fact that no one had scored a hundred at Nottingham that summer on pitches considered a seamer's delight. Head groundsman Frank Dalling had worked on the Test wicket for two years without a match being played on it. Having cast an eye over the virgin track, renowned cricket writer and broadcaster E.W. Swanton thought a second spinner would make a difference, regarding Gleeson as 'the most dangerous spinner in the match', before observing the pitch had 'no abundance of grass left and with a sunny weekend should be good for two spinners on the last two days'.

England stayed with Norman Gifford and Ray Illingworth, Australia stuck with Gleeson as the specialist tweaker. Lord's was only England's second loss in 22 Tests under Illingworth's leadership. As a sign of their concern, the MCC had taken footage of Bob Massie's bowling in the Lord's Test, slowing it down to analyse it frame by frame. County bowlers also resorted to bowling around the wicket, trying to imitate Massie's approach.

Ray Illingworth won the toss on a drab morning and rolled his arm over, sending Australia into bat. Murmurs of surprise spread through the growing Nottingham crowd. When Snow and Lever began their opening spell, England spilled early chances but, after half an hour, Francis fell to Lever, moving too slowly to pull a short ball and spooning to Mike Smith wide of mid-on.

By lunch, Ian Chappell had survived two chances, the first on nine, then on 24. Tony Greig was again the culprit, getting both hands to an edge off D'Oliveira. Under thickening clouds with the ball moving in the air and off the pitch, the Australian captain was eventually caught at chest height by Knott off Snow for 34, pushing forward to a reasonable length ball. It was an uncomfortable flashback to the Perth Test of 1970 when Chappell struggled against the England quick. Greg Chappell flicked a Snow full toss gracefully through square leg to the boundary before Knott and Parfitt, in consecutive deliveries, put down difficult catches off Stackpole driving at Greig.

Stackpole passed 50 in just under three hours, adding 59 with Greg Chappell for the third wicket before Parfitt caught the younger Chappell off Snow. Australia lost its fifth wicket at 5pm when Edwards edged a straight ball from Snow behind. Walters' angular blade edged Snow to Parfitt for two. As Stackpole slowly moved through the 90s, he struggled to get Phil Tresidder's bet on him scoring a hundred out of his mind. Playing tentatively at a Greig outswinger, he pulled the bat away late, and Knott appealed while the rest of the slips cordon remained unmoved. Stackpole turned and barked at the slip cordon 'to settle down'.

Twelfth man Paul Sheahan arrived with drinks and advice. 'Just concentrate and get your hundred.' On 99, Stackpole squeezed the ball toward square leg, calling, 'Yes! No! Go back.' Marsh responded with his right arm raised. The fielder fumbled, and Stackpole completed the run. When Stackpole's five-and-a-half-hour stay ended on 114, edging Tony Greig to Parfitt at slip, Greig pounded the pitch with his fist.

'You're nothing but a Teddy bear,' Stackpole snarled at the South

African as he walked by. Greig fired back. Illingworth approached him to calm the situation. E.W. Swanton, unaware that Stackpole had started the heated exchange, reprimanded Greig in the press the next day, saying, 'We don't want South African bullying on the field'. The Australian opener's knock was crucial to his side's confidence, sending a message to his teammates that John Snow was playable even under challenging conditions. Australia reached 6 for 249 by stumps.

On the second day, with the sun out, Gifford enticed Marsh to loft to a running D'Oliveira at deep square leg. Marsh and Colley's 62-run partnership closed seven runs short of the Australians' record for the seventh wicket at Trent Bridge. Batting on off stump, Colley swung lustily across the line, swatting his way to 54 as Australia reached 315. The Australians looked more comfortable against Snow, but his 5 for 92 took his series wicket tally to 18. Despite the early fumbling in the slips, the jaunty Peter Parfitt became the eighth England player to hold four catches in an innings of an Ashes Test, joining Australians Sam Loxton and Neil Harvey. Parfitt bounded along with the appearance of a local butcher eagerly opening his shop to a bevy of customers, whatever the situation.

When England batted, Luckhurst played and missed at five of the first 14 balls he faced. Lillee entertained the crowd with a long and frantic run, steepling bouncers and pace, which often beat the batsman. The crowd jeered, at other times applauded. Luckhurst punched a short ball from Lillee through point, reaching double figures in two hours. Edrich, on seven, pulled Massie straight to Ross Edwards, standing five metres from the bat at short leg. Once again, the ball rebounded from Edwards' chest and hands as he dropped to his knees as the ball hit the turf. Luckhurst fell lbw in the last over before tea following Lillee's five stifling maidens in eight overs. Parfitt's half-forward step and lean into the ball wasn't enough to counter Massie's inswing castling his stumps. Edrich hooked Colley behind square leg and then tried again, top edging to Marsh, who ran ten metres to take the catch. Lillee continued his vaudeville act of slipping his false tooth (on a plate) in and out of his mouth as he walked back to bowl. His occasional full tosses had Marsh performing acrobatics behind the stumps, the keeper flinging his left glove down and rubbing his wrist. Two balls later, Marsh pouched a tumbling catch to his right off Snow. Lillee's 4 for 35 and Massie's 4 for 43 dismissed England for 189 in 396 minutes. Tellingly, of the last 30 England wickets to fall, Lillee and Massie had taken 28.

'Fire the flops or the Aussies will win 4–1', announced *People* (Mirror Group) in back-page headlines. Bruce Francis, suffering a migraine headache, was off the field for much of England's innings, causing Ross Edwards to approach his skipper and offer to open.

Ashley Mallett, watching on from the change room, thought Edwards was more badgering than asking, but Edwards argued that it was better to sacrifice him than move all the batsmen out of their positions. Chappell eventually agreed.

Edwards was no fool, he knew the pitch had flattened out and runs were to be made. He'd opened for Western Australia, and thought this might be a chance to cement his place in the Australian side. Proving how much the pitch had improved, Stackpole took nine off Snow's first three balls. When Stackpole edged a ball from Snow's second over, it gifted Luckhurst a stomach-height catch at first slip. Edwards and Ian Chappell then added 124 in 160 minutes before a sweep-happy Chappell was trapped in front by Illingworth. By stumps, Edwards, batting for 200 minutes, remained undefeated on 90. Sitting with his father, Eddie, in the Australian dressing room, Edward's beaming smile found the photographer's camera. Edwards couldn't believe his luck. 'I was a nobody they knew very little about. First, they concentrated on Stackpole, then Ian Chappell, then Greg Chappell and then Doug Walters and, all the while, I was nicking and nudging, and by the end of the day's play, no one noticed that I was 90 not out, except me.' Edwards had been getting into position early, moving just before the bowler let go of the ball instead of while playing a stroke. On the Sunday rest day, he spent the morning in his hotel room watching TV and listening to cassette tapes before wandering around Nottingham Castle. One sure thing was Western Australia's growing influence on the Australian side. WAFL footballer and reporter Austin Robertson led the chorus – 'How often has WA been called the Cinderella state of cricket?' After winning the Shield twice in four years (1968, 1972) Robertson declared, 'It was now clear that distance, population, facilities, past poor performances and a lack of tried and proven Test players had been overcome.'

Western Australia, as a cricketing state, was at the beginning of a period of dominance. Ian Brayshaw remembered: 'Barry Shepherd led the Renaissance with a "we can take them down attitude", Tony Lock taught us how to win, John Inverarity showed us how to keep winning . . . and later, Rod Marsh would teach "how to beat the shit out of the opposition".' Cartoonist Norm Mitchell highlighted the Western Australian's success in a cartoon showing two men driving behind a car emblazoned on the rear windscreen with the names and pictures of Massie, Lillee, Marsh and Edwards, as well as posters of the Sheffield Shield and the Footy Carnival runners up. The man driving the car following says, 'It's getting extremely embarrassing driving behind sandgropers' cars these days.'

With the series at one-all, the question of how England would blunt Massie's swing bowling was yet to be answered. A photo spread in the *Daily Mail* by club cricketer and fast bowling student Richard Gwynn claimed to have laid bare the secrets of Massie's swing. According to Gwynn, the clues to unlocking the outswinger were on delivery. Just before bowling, Massie's right hand rose in front of his body and close to his chin as he looked over his left arm. For the inswinger, Massie's right arm moved out from his body in an anticlockwise loop as he peered under his left arm, showing the batsman more chest. Simple, right? Richie Benaud promptly described the summary as 'nonsense'.

On the morning of the fourth day, the Australians toured the Nottingham Children's Hospital wards. The young patients didn't recognise the star cricketers, but the accompanying cameras excited them. Edwards paused for photos with Ian Chappell, Stackpole, Watson, Taber and Inverarity. Dave McErlane, with his 20 years of hospital experience, joined the group on the rounds. Teenager Jeremy Morley of Lowham was presented with tour memorabilia, parents, staff, and patients were given autographs.

By the time Edwards was back out in the middle of the Trent Bridge ground in bright and clear conditions, a crowd of 11,000 awaited. Beginning with a single off Gifford, he clipped Snow off his toes for two before following with a similar stroke off Lever for four. It took 17 minutes for Edwards to reach his century as he turned Snow to midwicket and sprinted for a single. The milestone had consumed 197 deliveries in almost four hours with nine boundaries. Edwards knew that England's bowlers had lost heart and that a big hundred was in the offing. As Illingworth pushed his fielders deeper, Edwards and Greg Chappell picked up singles. After batting for 27 minutes without getting off the mark, Greg Chappell (72) dominated the 146-run partnership with Edwards for the third wicket. Walters, chasing runs, loosely cut a long hop to Gifford running backwards in the covers, moving like an Australian Rules football umpire to take the catch. When Edwards pushed Illingworth for a single, Greig threw wildly, and Australia eased passed 300. By the time Ian Chappell declared, 20 minutes after lunch on day four, Edwards was 170 not out, with Australia 4 for 324. Edwards was the first Western Australian to score a Test century (overtaking Barry Shepherd's 96 in the Second Test v South Africa at Melbourne in 1963/64). England had nine-and-a-half hours to score 451.

Before England's innings, the former England and Nottinghamshire captain Reg Simpson ominously appeared in the Australian dressing room. Best known for his unbeaten 156 in 1951 at the MCG, Simpson had helped guide England to its first win in an Ashes Test match for almost 13 years. A former policeman and RAF pilot, who reached the rank of flight lieutenant, Simpson knew how to give orders. By 1972 he was a Gunn & Moore executive, chair of Nottinghamshire's CCC committee, and club president. Walking through the Australian dressing room, Simpson made a beeline for Ian Chappell, telling him, 'You're picking the wrong ball,' in reference to the choice of the new ball. 'I'm not picking the ball, mate; he is,' Chappell replied, pointing to Bob Massie sitting in the corner of the visitors' dressing room. Simpson repeated his claim to Chappell, who replied, 'Listen, mate, Massie picked the ball in both innings at Lord's and in the first innings at Trent Bridge, and he'll continue to pick the ball.' Simpson turned and walked with heavy footsteps out of the dressing room. The incident had Ian Chappell wondering what had happened. Years later, Tony Greig revealed that Simpson was working for Gunn & Moore as a cricket ball representative on a commission.

England batted again. Lillee's first ball was a bouncer to Luckhurst, surrounded by four slips and a gully. Another to Edrich landed chest height in Marsh's gloves. The lively bounce proved that the pitch, having flattened since the first day, still had some life. Massie changed ends, hoping that a cross-field breeze would enhance his outswing. After the euphoria of a Test hundred, Edwards had to leave the field when he injured a finger stopping a cover drive from Luckhurst. Paul Sheahan substituted while Edwards sat with his parents in the crowd.

Gone were the tentative prods and lack of footwork as Luckhurst finally began to bat with greater confidence. After 210 minutes, England was 1 for 111, with Edrich the only casualty, bowled by Massie for 15. Lillee wrapped Parfitt on the pads, who pointed to his bat, indicating he had edged the ball. Lillee was twice warned by umpire Albert 'Dusty' Rhodes for running on the pitch. It would have taken only one more warning to bar Lillee from bowling for the rest of the match (although, as Ian Chappell later found out, he could have continued to bowl him from the other end). Illingworth sent a message to Parfitt: 'For heaven's sake, stop those fellows running on the pitch.' Colley was also careless in following through but escaped the umpire's gaze. Chappell took Lillee off after the second warning, believing 'there was no point in busting himself when a draw looked certain'.

Indeed, Australia failed to break the back of the English batting. Gleeson bowled 30 wicketless overs, conceding just 49. Part of England's success in countering Australia's 'mystery spinner' was Alan Knott, who learned to bowl just like Gleeson but from 20 yards (18 metres) in the nets. It helped the English batsmen convince themselves that what looked like a leg spinner was actually an off spinner. When Gleeson delivered a genuine leg spinner to Illingworth he half-jokingly responded, 'Have you got a new one [delivery]?'

Ian Chappell eventually dismissed Luckhurst on 96, hitting across the line with the edge flying to Greg Chappell at second slip. Luckhurst and Parfitt added 117 in three-and-three-quarter hours, providing England's only century stand in the series. When Parfitt pushed forward defensively to Lillee on 46, the ball clipped the top of the off stump, ending the left-hander's 281-minute stay. D'Oliveira made his first half-century in 17 Test innings before Ian Chappell, using his captain's prerogative, led everyone back to the pavilion. The Australians had toiled for nine-and-a-half hours, taking just four wickets, a disheartening reminder of the ever-changing fortunes of the series. Illingworth believed England had let themselves down with the bat in the first innings but was satisfied with his decision to send Australia in.

> Had we held our catches and bowled as well as we should have, we would have got them out for 180 or 200. We also would have considered attempting a victory had we not lost a wicket before lunch [on the final day], but with the sudden departure of Luckhurst, Parfitt and Mike Smith it would have been foolish to go for the runs.

Given the flatness of the pitch, the explanation illustrates Illingworth's defensive frame of mind. Both captains had erred. Ian Chappell's failure to include Ashley Mallett instead of Gleeson was a mistake. Chappell and Keith Stackpole bowled 29 overs between them in the second innings.

England's defiant reply raised questions about the 'mystique' behind Massie's swing and Lillee's dominant pace. John Woodcock in *The Times* described a renewed batting strength and 'an important psychological victory'. Peter Laker's *Daily Mirror* article observed, 'The destroyers at Lord's are not super bowlers or supermen . . . only when they are allowed to intimidate.' The comment makes for interesting reading, hinting that the key to countering Lillee and Marsh lay mainly in the conditions.

The Australian's stay at Nottingham had its off-field controversy. Lillee and Massie received anonymous letters threatening the safety of their families. The mail posted in Sydney and received in Trent Bridge warned the bowlers not to take more than two wickets in the last two Tests. The handwritten letter to Lillee read, 'If you do not heed this warning, we will have to chop your mother'. A message to the Australian police only mentioned the threat to Massie, while the Perth CIB Superintendent A.J. Parker informed Massie's family and put protections in place. Ray Steele revealed the letters were handed to Interpol, although police were quick to dismiss the threats.

There was, however, one disturbing incident early on the rest day at Nottingham when two men arrived at the hotel looking to rough up Lillee. Having knocked on his hotel room door, they mistook roommate David Colley for Lillee. Colley thought the intruders were professional hit men. 'A couple of very big lads . . . who threw me around like a rag doll. I eventually managed to show them my passport to prove I wasn't Dennis.' Later, there was a scuffle in the hotel foyer when an elderly relief porter was pushed to the ground. Colley reflected on the night and the attackers. 'I don't think they were that bright . . . they waited across the road in a park where they were later picked up by the police.'

All the while, Lillee was enjoying his evening at the bar, completely unaware of the fracas. Colley recalls Lillee telling him that 'he could have taken them both on'. Steele, imperturbable as always, described it as 'a storm in a teacup'. Soon, the incident passed as if it had never happened. The press played it down, only the AAP producing a brief article mentioning a scuffle in which a porter was injured by thugs seeking Lillee.

Bruce Francis was in pain of a different type. Sometimes Francis was the butt of teammates' friendly jokes but he was now copping more than usual. When the Australians fielded on day two, Francis started chatting with some English girls watching from the edge of the boundary. After play, he discovered they were the England players' wives and girlfriends. Francis' day three migraine was also the topic of some leg pulling. 'Very costly headache, Bruce,' one commented. For the Australians, there would continue to be surprises around every corner. Despite the success at Trent Bridge, Rudyard Kipling's sage advice of treating triumph and disaster as the same would soon ring loudly in Ross Edwards' ears.

Chapter Eight
Leeds awaits

The Australians' hectic schedule continued apace. In the 24 hours following the Third Test, they drove to Longton at Stoke-on-Kent to face the Minor Counties, a cricket league below the status of a county game that mainly played two-day non-first-class fixtures. It may seem odd that such a match was scheduled, but it had long been a tradition (since 1878) that the visiting Australians play a Minor County. In 1926, the Herbie Collins-led Australian side played a two-day fixture against Durham, attracting a first-day crowd of 26,000 and gate money of £2000 for the match (worth £153,000 today).

After nine-and-a-half hours in the field during the Test, the Australians were relieved when Keith Stackpole won the toss and batted. In front of a crowd in the hundreds, Watson finished five short of his second hundred of the tour, while Inverarity, batting at number four, completed an undefeated century. Australia declared at 5 for 325. Jeff Hammond took 6 for 15 from 15.2 overs, routing the opposition for 161, finishing the match a day early.

Four weeks had passed since Hammond began working harder on his fitness. The sumptuous feasts available at the seemingly never-ending functions the Australians attended and the lack of match play had added weight where it wasn't needed and reduced his stamina.

Hammond was a quiet tourist, really a boy among men. He didn't say much and admired the extra physical work done by Dennis Lillee away from team practices. Hammond recalled a moment sitting on the team bus believing that his tour was slipping by, 'I thought, hang on sunshine, you'd better get off your arse and start doing some extra work.' When based at the Waldorf Hotel, Hammond set himself the task of running through the streets of London each morning and night. When he was the twelfth man for Australia (he missed 13 games out of 27, although five were Tests), he used the time effectively, bowling with more intent in the nets. He adapted his bowling to suit the conditions, learning to move the ball off the pitch and swing it. Lillee and Massie helped guide him during casual conversations at the bar. When Hammond played the Minor Counties, he was confident that his renewed approach was working. Behind the scenes Stackpole was also encouraging the young South Australian 'to keep at it'.

Gleeson regained some confidence against Minor Counties after experimenting with flight; he took three first-innings wickets, while Mallett's sharp-turning off breaks captured 4 for 13. The Australians' victory by an innings and 26 runs meant an early finish, which gave the team some free time. Hammond continued entertaining his teammates, trying his hand at the local pottery, impressing John Gleeson, Ashley Mallett and Bob Massie with his work.

Ian Chappell later wrote that one of the keys to the success of the touring side lay in the performances of those not in the Test side, by laying claims to a Test position. The little-used Brian Taber was an example with his seven dismissals in the game against the Minor Counties.

Awaiting the start of the Fourth Test, Ian Chappell and Rod Marsh enjoyed the Wimbledon ambiance, where they spoke with Lew Hoad, Neale Fraser and Evonne Goolagong, revelling in the latter's win in the semi-final against Chris Evert. They also admired Ilie Nastase's form against Clark Graebner, as the Romanian worked toward the final.

Jeff Hammond passed on the news that the two-Test Pakistan batsman Younis Ahmed was signed to play for Prospect (Hammond's club in Adelaide) and had Ian Chappell bristling. Chappell didn't rate

Ahmed, who the Australians had encountered when they played Surrey. He also didn't appreciate that Sir Donald Bradman, then Chairman of Selectors for the South Australian Cricket Association, hadn't consulted him. Chappell decided the matter could wait. It was part of Chappell's strength as a captain to be able to compartmentalise when matters niggled away.

By July 1972, tensions between the British Army and the IRA were at boiling point. That year, one violent incident followed another, with a cycle of retribution soon following. On Sunday 30 January (Bloody Sunday), the British Army, believed to have come under fire, fatally shot 14 civilians and wounded 13 more during a civil rights march in Derry. On one day, the IRA exploded 23 bombs over Northern Ireland. Belfast became a war zone. By mid-July, the 100th British soldier had been killed, this time by a sniper in Belfast.

Ian Chappell's Australian coach headed to Hove three days later. As the tourists prepared to return to the bus after the meal at a motorway service area, the Australian team masseur, Dave McErlane, noticed Ray Steele still sitting, by himself, with a bulky briefcase. Naïvely (or stupidly), McErlane winked and smiled at the waitress, saying, 'See that bloke over there with the bald head and the glasses? He's got a bomb in his bag.' The Australians soon found themselves surrounded by army commandoes wearing flak jackets, submachine guns draped across their chests. Ray Steele and Ian Chappell talked their way out of the situation and the Australians were allowed to go, but only after hundreds of autographed team sheets were given to the army commander as an appreciation of understanding.

'A relaxed encounter' is how the local press described the Australians' clash with Sussex at Hove. Snow conceded 43 runs in 14 overs, failing to claim a wicket on the opening day. Edwards clubbed 41 while Ian Chappell hooked his way to 58 in 75 minutes with a six that landed on the betting marquee. Marsh's 54 included several strokes that sent the crowd in deck chairs scrambling at long-on. Sheahan pulled Michael

Buss over midwicket, hitting the roof of the stand and bouncing into the shrubbery of an adjacent garden. Ashley Mallett and Jeff Hammond batted for the first time since May, adding 46 for the tenth wicket. Buss bowled a combination of medium pace and slow left-arm orthodox spin, taking 5 for 69, while Sussex edged past Australia's 294 with five wickets down before declaring. Opener Geoff Greenidge nervously fell for 99 when Ian Chappell enticed an edge to Marsh. Stackpole became the first Australian to reach 1000 runs on the tour after he swung a ball from Buss to the midwicket fence. Riding his luck, the Australian deputy moved to his third century of the tour before finishing with an undefeated 154.

By the end of the third day, Sussex became the first county to defeat the 1972 Australians, winning by five wickets. It was the first time they had defeated the Australians since 1888. Geoff Greenidge's second innings 125 included a century opening stand with Peter Graves (48) and a partnership with Roger Prideaux, adding 89 in 49 minutes. Although Mallett took only two wickets for the match, Richie Benaud's syndicated column argued for his inclusion in the Fourth Test.

A one-day match to mark Sussex ground's centenary celebration lasted only 30 minutes before rain washed out play. Ian Chappell watched on with a smile at the Hove clubrooms when former England captain Arthur Gilligan received a portrait of himself. Gilligan, then president of the MCC, had been a great friend (and co-commentator) of Chappell's grandfather, Vic Richardson. During the 1950s and 60s, Richardson's often repeated phrase – 'And what do you think, Arthur?' – became part of the Australian vernacular for a while.

Ian Chappell asked Paul Sheahan if he would like to be considered as an opener for the Fourth Test at Leeds. Sheahan's middle-order undefeated 135 against Leicester before the Third Test complemented his 67 against the Minor Counties batting at number three, and his 50 in the second innings against Sussex. As it was, Ross Edwards opened and Sheahan batted at number five.

Sheahan, the great-grandson of former Australian player William Cooper, had come to the baggy green from a rich cricketing pedigree. He had promised much since scoring 202 against South Australia in 1966/67. He'd toured England in 1968 as a 21-year-old, scoring 809 runs at 28, but failed to live up to expectations.

Ian Chappell, Jeff Hammond and Graeme Watson enjoyed the local nightlife at Hove. So much so that driving home after a night out, they hit a few golf balls onto an open field on their way back to the hotel. Trouble loomed. Seeing the lights of the expressway, Ian Chappell drove towards it, accidentally pitching the car into a ditch. The trio's walk back proved quieter than usual as they wondered how they'd explain the incident to team management. 'Would you believe me if I told you the car was stolen?'

'No,' came the reply.

'That's it. The last time I'm driving in this fucking country,' said Chappell as he threw the car keys on the table.

The English summer of 1972 had so far proven a paceman's delight. Snow, Massie and Lillee had taken 60 wickets between them in the first three Tests. Eight days after the Sussex clash, the Australians caught the train from London's King's Cross station to Leeds. Unsurprisingly, they expected a green seamer's pitch and similarly lush outfield for the Fourth Test. Historically, Australia had a superior record to England at Leeds in their 14 Tests against each other since 1899. The tally stood at Australia's five wins, England's two, and seven drawn. England's two wins over the 73 years – in 1956 and 1961 – both played on pitches unfit for Test cricket and advantageous to the home side.

Doug Walters' poor form continued to be one of the mysteries of his career. He was a swashbuckling, indomitable force in Australia against England but struggled in conditions where the ball moved off the pitch. Walters' long looping angular back lift made him prone to playing across the line and edging to the gully or slips. His scores in his previous seven Tests in England of 26, 0, 46, 56, 5, 1, 17, 20, 1, 2 and 7 for 223 runs at 18.75 were indications that Walters' inclusion for Leeds was more Ian Chappell's continuing faith in him than evidence of form. Chappell knew, though, that Walters had a rare ability to turn a match with his explosive batting skills. In short, he was a match winner, and they were hard to find. England made five changes, with Smith, Lever and Gifford dropping out, along with Hampshire and Hutton (who were summoned to Nottingham to join the squad). The newcomers included Michael John Smith, Keith Fletcher, Chris Old and Derek Underwood; Geoff Arnold returned from injury. Middlesex opener Smith's inclusion was more a precautionary move after Edrich injured a stomach muscle during the Third Test. When the final side was selected, England, for the first time since 1921, played without a single member of the current Yorkshire side.

Chapter Nine

Fourth Test, Headingley

When the Australians arrived at Leeds to play the crucial Fourth Test of the series, the centre square of the ground mystified all who saw it. Richie Benaud had watched Yorkshire play Warwickshire in the Gillette Cup three weeks earlier, on a pitch and ground lush green, enabling Bob Willis to bowl a sharp lifter, which broke Geoff Boycott's finger. At the time, Benaud wondered what Lillee might do on the well-grassed pacy surface. With Leeds' industrial centre nearby and the ground set in a basin, a heavy atmosphere hovered above. Players mainly knew what they would get when they played at Leeds, a pacy seaming wicket that was decidedly lively on the first day.

Twenty-four hours before the first ball was bowled, Keith Stackpole suggested to Ian Chappell that he might want to closely examine the pitch.

'I only look at the pitch on the first morning of the match,' was the captain's terse reply.

'Well, you'd better have a look at this one.'

A knowing look from Stackpole was met with a raised eyebrow from Chappell when the pair arrived in the centre. The pitch was damp, the grass cut away to the roots. A rainstorm had blown through Manchester five days before (not unusual even at the end of July). Stackpole threw a ball hard into the pitch's surface and watched as the ball 'bounced' to toe height.

'Watch this,' he said to his skipper as he pounded the ball into the lush green strip next to the pitch, and the ball bounced close to chest height. Stackpole walked back to the match pitch and pressed his finger into it. The pitch's surface wobbled like jelly. Soon, other Australian players were pounding practice balls into the turf before walking away in disbelief. Not one of the balls had bounced. The Australian press watched from the press box, not quite believing what they saw. Mallett remembered the Leeds outfield was lush green but the 20 metres in the middle 'looked like a chook patch'. Once he saw the pitch, Ian Chappell knew it would be low, slow and difficult to bat on. His initial thought was the game would be a dull draw.

Mike Coward could barely believe his eyes as he stared at the verdant carpet across the ground before focusing on the bare discoloured strip in the middle. The Australians now realised why Derek Underwood had been suddenly called into the side. Kent's twirling left-arm orthodox spinner's summer so far had been one of limited opportunity and modest results, with 13 wickets in six first-class matches for Kent. Gifford, who he was to replace, had taken just one wicket in the series. John Inverarity thought of the final session at The Oval in 1968 when, in just his second Test, he had prodded and poked at Underwood on a wet pitch for 45 minutes before finally succumbing, padding up to a faster ball. Underwood's ability to bamboozle on a wet pitch (no matter the game's state) was well known. His captain at Kent, Mike Denness, knew that if it rained overnight during a match, he would 'sleep comfortably knowing the opposition would be bowled out cheaply the next day'. Ian Chappell needed spinners in the side but John Gleeson wouldn't be one of them. In three matches, he'd taken just three Test wickets at 52; Gleeson also needed a much faster, harder surface to be effective. Ten-test player Ashley Mallett was back in the Australian side for the first time since being dropped after two Tests against England in 1970/71. As his state captain, Ian Chappell knew Mallett's value and what fields he needed to set for the tall, rangy off spinner to be effective. Chappell also had faith in the spinning wiles of

John Inverarity, who he saw as 'a more than useful left-arm orthodox on a turning pitch'. Inverarity's four wickets in Sussex's second innings took his wicket tally to 30 on tour, and he had proved to be an adept close-in fieldsman. Paul Sheahan had done enough to appear in his 26th Test.

Adding to the concerns were the unusable damp practice wickets. The Australians again had to use the outfield for throw-downs and fielding practice in preparation for a Test match on a pitch that was utterly foreign to them. For some, the relentless grind of the tour was also taking its toll. Greg Chappell needed dental treatment for the third time in as many days. A bottom tooth was removed, but not the abscessed one that had bothered him at Hove. Australia's premier batsman looked pale when he arrived at the Leeds ground to join his teammates. Ray Steele soon told the curious press that Greg Chappell was playing.

A large crowd gathered early and was seated long before the captains appeared in the middle of the ground. Ian Chappell won the toss for the first (and only) time in the series and chose to bat. It was the fifth toss in 17 matches he had called correctly, and batting was the only option. Under typically gloomy skies, Stackpole struck two boundaries from the opening over from Arnold before Edwards nicked Snow outside off stump to a diving Knott without scoring. Stackpole was missed on 21 by Fletcher throwing himself wide of first slip, but the stocky opener reached his half-century before lunch (his fifth of the series). Australia sat comfortably at 1 for 79 at the break, but the score was deceptive. The pitch was playing slow and low, and the prodigious turn had yet to begin. After 18 overs of play, Illingworth bowled three probing overs from the rugby ground end. At one o'clock, Illingworth replaced himself with Underwood, who bowled unchanged until the new ball was taken at ten past five.

The rot started for the Australians, when Stackpole pushed at a ball from Underwood edging to Knott (who, despite it brushing the off bail, took the catch). Mallett remembered the shocked reaction in the Australian dressing room. 'Underwood was bowling real medium pace to Stacky and Knott was taking balls over his head. The next one rose about six inches, and Knott caught it. It was the best piece of keeping I'd ever seen.' For the Chappells, batting was claustrophobic, with four men clustered around the bat, all within three metres. Parfitt at slip, Fletcher at short gully, Illingworth at silly mid-off and Luckhurst at short leg. Snow and Underwood conceded just six runs in the first 27 minutes after lunch. Ian Chappell managed two in 40 minutes before he was caught and bowled by Illingworth for 26. Having batted for 46 overs, the Australian captain had rarely been so subdued. When the score reached 93, a quicker ball from Underwood saw Greg Chappell caught in front, stumbling across the crease. At 5 for 98, Marsh, deciding that attack was the best option, tried to hit Underwood over long-on and skied the ball to Illingworth at mid-on. Sheahan fell for nought, and Australia had lost their last five wickets for five runs off 58 balls. Sheahan hovered for 33 minutes before prodding forward to Underwood and Illingworth held a spectacular one-handed catch at silly mid-off at the second attempt. Sheahan remembered his disappointment: 'I had enormous problems playing Underwood's left-arm orthodox tweakers, which used to give me a hell of a time because I was too willing to prop onto the front foot.'

For most of the day, it looked as if the Australians had been hypnotised. After they slumped to 7 for 98, Inverarity, undefeated on 26, and Mallett (20) showed resistance by putting on 47 in 80 minutes before Australia succumbed for 146. The scores read more like a series of English winter temperature forecasts than an Australian top order: Edwards 0, Greg Chappell 12, Walters 4, Sheahan 0, and Marsh 1.

Inverarity thought, 'The ball turned square and bounced ankle height . . . the conditions were foreign compared to anything we had experienced.' Australia's weakness against top-flight spin on a difficult pitch had been exposed. Ian Chappell didn't think anyone could have played Underwood well on that pitch. Underwood bowled 31 overs, taking 4 for 37, while Illingworth's two wickets in 21 overs leaked 32 runs. By the end of the first day, Edrich and Luckhurst had made 43 without loss.

Fingleton expressed his disappointment in his newspaper column, revealing how he interviewed George Cawthray (Leeds groundsman) the Tuesday before the match. Cawthray told him that the preparation for the Test was 'no different to any other'. On the first day, Fingleton mentioned the abnormal spin to Yorkshire secretary Joseph Lister. 'We'll wait and see how the Englishmen handle this pitch,' Lister replied. The exchange ended sourly when Fingleton said, 'Australia have no Underwood or Illingworth.' Lister walked away.

It took little time on the second day for Luckhurst to be caught one-handed by Greg Chappell diving forward at silly mid-on off Mallett for 18. Twenty minutes later, Lillee had Parfitt sparring at a ball that passed between bat and pad. Marsh comfortably took the catch, leaning back and throwing the ball high in the air in triumph. Parfitt walked from the ground like he'd just been pickpocketed. Fletcher was trapped on the back foot when Mallett went around the wicket, having tentatively made five in 26 minutes. Massie struggled to break through, slumping his shoulders in disappointment between overs. After over two hours at the crease, Edrich (45) lost patience and tried to loft Mallett only to find a running Ian Chappell at mid-off take a difficult catch. Mallett then delivered a flatter, faster and turning ball that skittled D'Oliveira. Four balls later, Marsh whipped off the bails with Knott short of his ground.

Illingworth took 50 minutes to score his first two runs while Sheahan covered the outfield like a gazelle. At one point, he athletically strode ten deep into the crowd (seated between the pickets and the rope) after trying to stop the ball from reaching the boundary. Greig became Inverarity's first wicket in Test cricket when he was brilliantly caught by a diving Greg Chappell at silly mid-on for 24. Inverarity enthusiastically swung his arms repeatedly and clapped in celebration. Inverarity's 12 overs included eight maidens. England had crashed from none for 43 overnight to 7 for 128. Snow survived an lbw appeal off Inverarity before being dropped on the boundary by Massie off Mallett. When Illingworth struck Mallett over mid-off, England took the lead. A pull shot for six meant Mallett had conceded 19 runs off his last three overs after taking 5 for 85. By 3 pm, Mallett had tired after bowling from the rugby ground end all day, delivering 28 consecutive overs. Ian Chappell bowled in tandem with his brother Greg before bringing Lillee back to take the second new ball, frequently beating the batsmen. By tea, England had scrambled to 7 for 191 before Snow missed a leg-side full toss from Inverarity and was stumped by Marsh one-handed, ending a 104-run partnership in three hours. Illingworth moved to 54 by on-driving Mallett for six, ending a day in which the England captain had played a significant role.

The Australians struggled to break through. Snow and Illingworth had batted with greater confidence than the Australians on a difficult pitch, and England finally reached 263. As Richie Benaud noted, 'The real condemnation of this pitch is that Inverarity was allowed to bowl 30 overs and take three wickets for 25.' Although he failed to make a vital breakthrough to close the England innings, Mallett's five-wicket haul justified his selection.

When Australia batted again, it took one ball for Ross Edwards to experience the humiliation of a pair in Test cricket, caught down the leg side off Arnold. 'I was numb. I couldn't do anything about it. I was just numb all day', he wrote in his diary that night. After Ian Chappell was drawn forward and caught behind for a duck off Arnold, Paul Sheahan walked out to bat amid a raucous Leeds crowd, knowing it was his 'make-or-break moment'. Sheahan vowed not to prop forward to Underwood but attack instead. The tactic worked when he drove and swept two early boundaries. By the time Australia collapsed to be all out for 136, Sheahan had scored an undefeated 41. The rout took just 56 overs. Underwood captured 6 for 45, giving him a match tally of 10 wickets. Edrich was then dispatched by Lillee before chasing down the 21 for a nine-wicket victory. The Fourth Test had lasted just short of two-and-a-half days.

After play, Stackpole sat in the Australian dressing room regretting his attacking second innings dismissal for 28. He'd swept at Underwood with his front foot down the pitch. The ball flicked his knee roll and flew over Knott's head. 'I started running and was halfway down when David Constant gave me out.' Had Stackpole survived and Australia batted an hour longer, the match could have ended in a draw; heavy rain followed immediately after the game ended. Constant later admitted that he might have erred in giving Stackpole out lbw.

The match's outcome left a deep impression on the players. Stackpole and Mallett engaged in a discussion about the equal significance of Alan Knott's wicketkeeping and Underwood's bowling. The match-winning stand of 104 by Snow and Illingworth also weighed heavily on the Australians. Stackpole's belief that 'if they could do it then we should have been able to do it' reflected the team's disappointment. The subpar Leeds pitch was a topic of discussion, with Ray Steele clarifying that the official pitch report from Australia wouldn't be a form of protest. However, in the privacy of the Australian dressing room, the sentiment was different, expressing a mix of disappointment and determination. 'We were dudded, we all know that, but we won't be whingeing about it to anyone, least of all the press. If anyone whines about the Headingley wicket I'll come down on you like a ton of bricks.'

Former Australian cricketer and commentator Jack Fingleton lashed out at the England cricket authorities in an after-dinner speech at the Queens Hotel where the Australians were staying. He claimed, 'The pitch at Leeds looked like so much grass had been taken from it that the top soil may have been disturbed as it was at Old Trafford in 1956 [the pitch on which Laker took 19 wickets].'

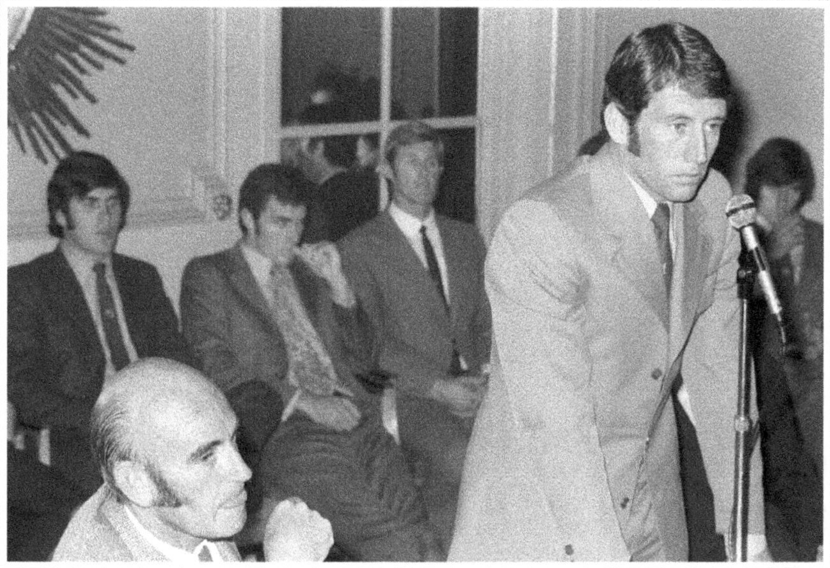

'We are here to play attacking cricket.'

Ian Chappell introduces his side to the British Press at the Waldorf Hotel. A jet-lagged David Colley, Greg Chappell, Ross Edwards, and Graeme Watson look on.

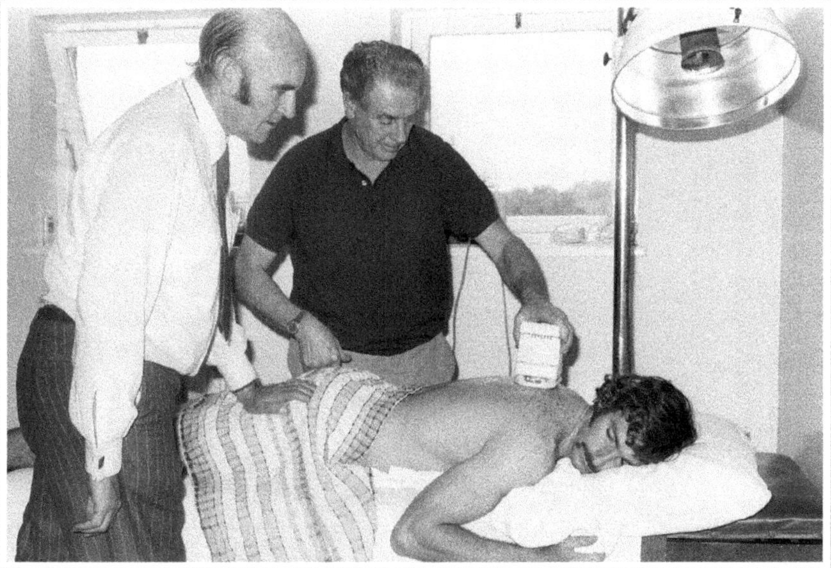

'One step forward, two steps back.'

Ray Steele watches as team physiotherapist Dave McErlane treats Dennis Lillee's troublesome back. Early in the tour, Lillee's back was so bad that he feared he would be sent home.

'A seamer's paradise.'

Team manager Ray Steele and the Australian vice-captain Keith Stackpole watched the final preparations for the pitch at Old Trafford.

Geoff Boycott is LBW to John Gleeson for 47 during the First Test. Rod Marsh and Keith Stackpole join in the chorus of appeal.

'Rain without rain.'

Ian Chappell and Ray Illingworth check the leaden skies as they prepare to toss for the Second Test at Lord's.

Not quite the weather for mini-skirts.

A chilly June morning greets Kensington model and programme seller Jilli Wale on the sold-out first day of the Second Test at Lord's, 22 June 1972.

England applies the pressure as Greg Chappell edges toward a majestic century in Australia's first innings of the Lord's Test.

Ray Illingworth hits Ashley Mallett for six on the second day of the Leeds Test. His innings of 57 proved crucial in England's win on the Fusarium-affected pitch.

A 1970s version of multi-tasking.

The Oval's groundsman Robert Hilliard, 22, and his fiancee Sandra MacManson enjoy a chess game during a short break while working the scoreboard at the Fifth Test.

The turning point of Australian cricket – Victory at The Oval.

The Australians – Ross Edwards, David Colley, Paul Sheahan, Rod Marsh, Jeff Hammond, Dennis Lillee, Graeme Watson – celebrate their win in the Fifth Test at The Oval.

'Anyone but England.'

West Indian cricket fans throw their support around the Australians at The Oval, August 1972

'My most significant Test win.'

Australian captain Ian Chappell takes a bottle of champagne from the ice bath while drinking a can of beer to toast a crucial win at The Oval – ensuring Australia drew the series.

After Fingleton spoke, Ian Chappell reflected on an encounter four years earlier when he was called into the press box after play. 'It was a county game, and Fingleton spent twenty minutes telling me how good a player he thought my brother Greg (who was playing for Somerset) was. I was half expecting a "well done" from Fingleton on the hundred I scored. Fingleton ended the conversation abruptly by saying, "By the way, Ian, never trust the English."' Ian Chappell was in no doubt that he meant the administrators, not the players.

Illingworth, who had scored a first innings 57, dryly observed, 'Wickets with grass and seamers are used all the time, and nothing is said. But when the wicket turns, there is a hue and cry.' Umpire Charlie Elliott declared he'd make his customary pitch report to the authorities. England great Denis Compton was not so kind, describing the wicket as 'a disgrace to Test cricket'. In the *Sunday Express*, Compton noted, 'The desert-like strip was a direct contrast to the lush green grass on the remainder of the square and outfield'. Michael Melford in the *Sunday Telegraph* wrote,

> People who saw other matches played here during the past month on a reasonably grassed pitch had looked forward to an exciting, well-balanced five-day Test. As they stood beside the bare brown rectangle yesterday evening looking at the green of the rest of the square, many were asking why the grass was taken off . . . no doubt it happened through a series of accidents, but you would not have to be a very suspicious Australian to recall 1956 and other years when the crafty English have profited from a similar accident.

One-Test player Keith Slater, who had played Lancashire League cricket, wrote in the *West Australian* under the headline 'Funny things happen with English wickets': 'Did you too get the impression that the Fourth Test wicket at Headingley was too good [for the Englishmen] to be true . . . my own experiences in England suggest it is not beyond some curators to be swayed by patriotism' (although some Australian curators have done similar). Slater's suspicions were raised after speaking to Bert Flack, the Old Trafford curator of the 1956 dust bowl after Jim Laker bowled England to victory with 19 victims in the Test. Flack told Slater he was 'instructed' on the type of wicket to prepare. Illingworth remained undeterred, saying how he had argued for Gifford to be included.

> I told the selectors that I thought we should give Gifford a fair go because we'd played on seaming wickets so far, but the selectors went for Underwood. I think Gifford would have bowled Australia out on that pitch anyway. It was a wet pitch, though, and Derek was in a class of his own on a wet pitch.

Underwood told Mike Coward for the ABC documentary *Cricket in the '70s: The Chappell Era*:

> The pitch was a little bit browner, and I thought goodness there wasn't a growth of grass on there. And I thought this could turn a bit by the third day. It turned a little bit from day one. And I relished it. I loved seeing the back of that baggy green cap go to the pavilion . . . That wicket was a good one to bowl on. I'd like to carry that one around with me.

Australia's performance was, in some ways, a mystery. Only three years earlier, they defeated a top-flight Indian spin attack on turning pitches on the subcontinent.

It was immediately announced that Bert Lock, the former curator at The Oval, would carry out a pitch inspection for the MCC in the following two days. The pitch wasn't covered, and heavy rain soon turned it from a strip of dust into a mud heap, making any conclusions about the surface impossible. The Marylebone Cricket Club report was delayed until later in August. Club secretary Billy Griffith said, 'There is nothing to be said until the report is received and considered by the pitch sub-committee of the Test and County Cricket Board [TCCB].

This is unlikely to be until the middle of August.' Ian Chappell, in his match report to the MCC, gave the pitch an 'unfit' rating, the lowest possible score. The August report revealed the pitch had been infected with *Fusarium oxysporum* (a fungus which usually thrived at 24°C or higher). Somewhat incredulously, Norman Preston, in the 1973 *Wisden*, absolved the groundsman of blame. 'The disease spread while the covers were on during the deluge and killed much of the grass before the staff had an opportunity to treat it. It was established that mowing was in no way to blame.' Despite the below-standard pitch, there was little doubt that England had played better in the hostile conditions.

Paul Sheahan, who topped scored for Australia in the second innings, was sure the wicket was prepared to suit Underwood. He labelled the MCC report 'an extraordinary piece of obfuscation from the Poms. How can you say the pitch was struck down by this mystery grass disease when the centre square was as lush as your front lawn? I had no idea that Fusarium struck on 22 yards'. Edwards thought the pitch 'obviously doctored and turned square, not that it affected me'. His main memory of the match was getting champagne caught in his throat when drinking it in the England dressing after the game and regretting the lost chance of the $10,000 on offer to the team to win back the Ashes. Inverarity saw the Australians as being 'cold stark dudded, causing a lot of pent-up emotion following the match'. When Inverarity later coached in England, he was surprised that 'terrific young men thought it was OK to change the conditions to your advantage. I was incredulous'. The disaster for Australia conjured a memory of the time Ian Chappell met Bert Flack, the curator of the 'dust bowl' at Old Trafford in 1956. In 1963, Chappell played one game for Lancashire against Cambridge University at Old Trafford. Then an unknown, Chappell spoke to Flack before the game who admitted the 1956 pitch was 'a fookin' turner all right'.

Despite the angst the match caused the Australians they didn't lose faith in their ability. Chappell made certain that his side maintained a single-minded and positive approach. For Ashley Mallett the Leeds Test was the defining point of his tour. Although he would have liked to take more wickets, Mallett knew he was on his way.

The early end to the Test saw the Australians explore Leeds as well as the Moortown Golf Club. To lift their mood Ross Edwards and John Inverarity visited an old schoolfriend in Harrogate in North Yorkshire before setting off to fish for trout. Edwards later joined Marsh at the St Peters bat factory where they discussed becoming sale reps in Australia. Lillee, Massie and Mike Coward took to the cinema to watch Barbra Streisand in *What's up Doc?* The following day the lure of St Andrews golf course was enough for Ian Chappell to plan to head north to Scotland independently. Some of the squad had already taken the team bus from Leeds to Manchester before boarding flight BE4582 to Edinburgh en route to a two-day game against Scotland in Perth. Ian Chappell's plans went awry after missing his early morning wake-up call so St Andrews would have to wait. A lack of accommodation back in London meant another night in Leeds staying at the Fitzwilliam Hotel where he bumped into Geoff Boycott, but few words were spoken. The next day Chappell flew to London where Inverarity, Rod Marsh and Ross Edwards had also travelled to meet their wives. Edwards had at least some good news after his pair at Leeds. He was announced as the *West Australian*'s Sports Star of the month in July, sponsored by Caltex Oil (Aust) Pty Ltd. What was certain was that Chappell, having lifted his side's morale after the loss at Old Trafford, would need to do so again.

Chapter Ten

Road to recovery

Sitting on the banks of the River Tay, Perth, in Scotland's east, not far from Edinburgh and Glasgow, provided a contrast and some scenic relief for the Australians after the tumult of the Leeds Test match. The town, nestled between two large public parks and surrounded by Georgian townhouses, cobbled streets and medieval spires, allowed the Australians a break from the hustle and bustle of the large industrial city they had travelled from. The tradition of an Australian side taking the high road to the north to play the Scots dates back to 1880, with the previous fixture in Aberdeen in 1964 ending in a draw.

The Australians' second-class game at Perthshire Cricket Club at North Inch, a spacious ground, provided an opportunity to refresh the batteries and experience a six-wicket win in two days. Mallett and Gleeson helped bowl Scotland out for 159 in the first innings and 78 in the second, taking 12 wickets between them. Bruce Francis scored a carefree 58 as Australia declared at 8 for 142 before quickly chasing the target of 96. Walters' scores of 9 and 0 did little to restore his confidence, even against a second-string attack.

Arriving in Northampton after a tiring five-hour coach journey south, the Australians were determined to bounce back. The match against Northamptonshire and Indian import Bishan Bedi was seen as a chance to practice against left-arm orthodox spin. Despite the surprise decision to name a relatively weak batting side, with Greg Chappell, Stackpole and Sheahan left out, the team remained focused.

Bedi's five first inning wickets, and four in the second, at 12 runs apiece, proved challenging for Australia, which managed only 191 and 143. Rod Marsh's first innings 42 and Graeme Watson's second innings 52 were the few highlights for the tourists.

The Australians wondered at the front-foot style of David Steele (60) as he put on 64 with Mushtaq Mohammed (30) during Northamptonshire's successful second innings run chase. Mushtaq was backing up his first innings quickfire 88 in Northants, totalling 210, when Dennis Lillee was warned for the first time on tour for bowling excessive bouncers. His four short balls in seven deliveries had respected ten-year county umpire John Arnold walking down the pitch wagging his finger. Bob Massie needed manipulative treatment for a neck injury and was supervised by Lillee's orthopaedic surgeon, Alun Thomas, who had earlier overseen Massie's recovery from an abdominal muscle strain. Graeme Watson provided a reminder he could nip the ball off the pitch with surprising pace in finishing with 5 for 36. Brian Taber was promised the last over to bowl, but when Colley had his first two deliveries struck for boundaries, the reserve keeper missed his chance. The tourists lost by seven wickets after struggling to cope with a slow pitch and crafty bowling by Bedi, confirming a weakness against quality left-arm orthodox spin.

A ball-tampering allegation caused a stir in the Australian camp leading into the Fifth Test at The Oval. Former England captain Ted Dexter launched an extraordinary and ambiguous accusation in the *Sunday Mirror* under the headline 'Cricket Scandal and Exposed: The Shiny Ball Racket'. The Australians had no doubt about what he was saying and who he was aiming his comments at – Bob Massie's performance at Lord's.

Sounding more like an MI5 Agent than a former England captain, Dexter wrote,

> I thought I knew every dirty dodge in cricket. But bowlers in the first class game have come up with something new. The code

> name for their latest fiddle is 'lip-ice', a largely undetectable lip salve that helped swing the ball considerably.

Dexter also claimed to have approached Australian manager Ray Steele about using the salve, who supposedly 'put an end to it'. It's worth noting that Massie continued his success in the first innings at Trent Bridge (taking four wickets before being nullified by the Leeds pitch). If 'lip-ice' was widely used, why wasn't England able to swing the ball like Massie did at Lord's? England first-class bowlers were adept at ball tampering in county cricket. Bob Woolmer once claimed that every English first-class bowler he faced between 1968 and 1984 tampered with the ball.

Despite the controversy, it was soon onto The Oval and the chance for Australia to level the series. Keith Stackpole confided in journalist Graham Eccles that he and Inverarity wanted to drop Doug Walters. The frank exchange between the Australian vice-captain and Eccles reveals much about the relationship between players and the press in the early 1970s.

Although the rubber was officially dead, there was much riding on the last game for the Australians. The final Test loomed critical for Ian Chappell for his captaincy, and a win would indicate progress. Given the intense interest in the series, the TCCB announced that the Fifth Test would be played over six days. Perhaps the move provided a greater chance of a fair result after the Leeds debacle. Ray Illingworth disagreed with scheduling the extra day's play, given that the series had already been decided. As John Arlott wrote: 'Only once – at the Oval in 1930, when rain prevented any play on the fifth day – has a Test in England lasted to the sixth day.' The Gillette Cup semi-finals were moved forward a day in anticipation of the match going into the sixth day.

Keith Fletcher and Brian Luckhurst were omitted from the England line-up, with Lancashire opener Barry Wood and Yorkshire top order batsman John Hampshire coming in. The blond-haired, short and stocky 29-year-old Barry Wood had impressed the Australians early in the tour, averaged more than 40 in county cricket, and was a useful medium-pace bowler and a fine close-to-the-wicket fieldsman. The Australians encountered the 31-year-old John Hampshire at home in 1970/71, where he struggled against Lillee, who dismissed him once and had him dropped three times.

Ian Chappell and his co-selectors huddled together on the fringe of The Oval centre square for an hour, discussing the best make-up of the side for the final Test. Doug Walters was pivotal to the conversation. He had to go after scoring just 54 Test runs at an average of 7.71 and failing to reach 50 in an innings in the previous two months. Ian Chappell told Walters before the team dinner that he was omitted from the side for the final Test. 'I believe he deserved that much for his service to Australian cricket.'

That night when the team was announced, Walters, as a joke, borrowed a pair of glasses mimicking Ray Steele (after the Old Trafford Test) and held up a newspaper with the headline 'Take this lying down . . . Pig's bloody arse we will'.

'There seemed to be a let's do it for Dougie attitude among the side,' Chappell observed. Australia was on a losing streak, losing its previous three first-class matches by five wickets to Sussex, nine to England and seven to Northamptonshire. After a run-less Leeds Test, Ross Edwards dropped down the order while Graeme Watson, coming off a second-inning half-century at Northampton, opened. Steele thought the Australians had relaxed after the 'big letdown in the Fourth Test', and now saw the need for the side to 'knuckle down . . . I think they are good enough to win and prove a point'. Talking to the press, Ian Chappell highlighted that England was making more changes to their side than the Australians despite leading the series before adding that 'England had had yet to reach 300 in an innings'.

Chapter Eleven

Fifth Test, The Oval

On the first morning of the final Test of the summer fans alighted from trains at the Vauxhall tube station, and lined up outside The Oval while newspaper boys squawked their wares in the glorious sunshine. Australia went into a Test match for the first time without a New South Welshman in the side. The move finally put paid to the idea that 'when New South Wales cricket is strong, Australian cricket is strong'. The power shift had moved west. The Australian line-up included six Western Australians, three South Australians, and two Victorians. The makeup of the Australian side provided a landmark for Western Australian cricket: the first time the state had six players in the Test squad of 12. 'A tribute to WA cricket,' said the WACA vice-president Frank Bryant. It was a far cry from the 1968 tour when Graham McKenzie was the only sandgroper in the touring party.

Dennis Lillee knew that The Oval pitch would have pace and bounce. It had only been a year since he played as a professional for Haslingden in the Lancashire League, but to Lillee it seemed a lifetime ago. The season had provided a turning point for Lillee, who realised that using the conditions to your favour was as crucial as bowling fast. For several months, he had excited crowds with a run that consisted of smooth acceleration, long pounding strides, fluid bowling action, control, the ability to move the ball off the pitch, and extreme pace. Frank Tyson wrote, 'When he [Lillee] arrived at the wicket, it looked as if he were about to deliver himself at the batsman's crease rather than the ball'.

By August 1972, less than two years since his debut, Dennis Lillee was a household name in England and such a force of nature on the field that he defied definition.

Mike Coward watched the Australians training on The Oval practice pitches unable to believe his luck. He was seated in the press box next to the famous broadcaster and journalist John Arlott. That summer, Coward had lapped up any chance to be in the company of journalists of the quality of Crawford White and John Woodcock, and struggled to contain his excitement when Keith Miller occasionally popped his head in to say hello. By August, Coward was also partly relieved the Test series was ending. As an agency man, he had barely stopped working, at one stage even helping to roll the pitch at a county game. Coward knew he'd again be busy during the Fifth Test and was grateful to have access to a copy boy (as he had for the Lord's Test). In a far cry from today's real-time reporting of matches, Coward typed his stories before phoning them to the copy boy, who read the text to the copytakers. Coward was close to the Australians and felt Chappell's growing sense of agitation over the number of fixtures his side had to play. Counties often rested their best players while reaping the financial benefits of hosting an Australian side. Despite the frustrations, Ian Chappell continued to lead and play, as Coward put it 'with a sense of willing enterprise'. That was just the Chappell way.

The Australians were in more familiar territory with the sun out, a dry and livelier pitch, and a lightning outfield. Ian Chappell lost the toss for the fourth time in the series and turned to Ray Illingworth, saying, 'Don't they make any coins with heads on them?' Illingworth smiled and chose to bat.

Lillee immediately roughed up the debutante Wood, striking him with a rising ball on the left arm. Caution preceded attack. Four runs were eked out in the first 28 minutes. Movement by spectators in front of the sightscreens at the Vauxhall End caused two stoppages, slowing the play even more. After just under an hour, Edrich shuffled across the crease and perished lbw to Lillee. Lumbering in, Graeme Watson gained extra pace and enticed Wood to edge behind for 26 on the cusp of lunch. England had ambled to 50 in 27 overs by the break.

After lunch, Parfitt pushed Lillee to Mallett at short mid-wicket and almost ran himself out. John Hampshire then showed class by pulling Massie to the boundary before driving him down the ground. Thirty-eight runs had flowed in 65 minutes. Mallett, using his height to his advantage, made the ball jump. Hampshire, with an ungainly cut, was caught by Inverarity at point for 42, ending a much-needed 83-run partnership with Parfitt. D'Oliveira prodded forward to Mallett, bat-padding to a diving Greg Chappell at short leg, who held the catch in an outstretched hand just above the ground. Mallett had taken 2 for 4 from seven balls. Lillee then uprooted Parfitt's middle stump for 51 before Illingworth was gleefully taken in the slips by Greg Chappell the next ball. Stackpole's suggestion of a third slip helped manufacture the dismissal, providing another example of the deputy's value as a tactician. England had lost four wickets for 12 and collapsed to 6 for 145. Mallett then bowled a ball that drifted toward the slips that Greig edged to Stackpole. Lillee again struck with Snow nicking to Marsh.

Alan Knott proved his worth with his measured defence and unconventional cross-bat swats. He batted with control and finesse against Mallett, Watson and Inverarity, but when Massie delivered around the wicket, Knott aggressively drove and cut three fours in an over. Knott's 81-run ninth wicket partnership in 69 minutes with Geoff Arnold ended when the England medium pacer was bowled by Inverarity.

Australia wrapped up England's innings when Knott (92) was caught behind off Lillee. England had reached 284 runs in 378 minutes, with Lillee finishing with 5 for 58 from 24.2 overs. Tour records tumbled. When Marsh caught Knott off Lillee, he created a record of 21 dismissals for Australian wicketkeepers in a five-Test series against England. Mallett had also bowled well in tandem with Lillee, snapping up the crucial first innings wickets of Hampshire, D'Oliveira, and Greig, finishing with 3 for 80.

Graeme Watson became Stackpole's third opening partner for the series. He began confidently with two blazing hooks before falling to a catch by Knott down the leg side for 13 from an authentic leg glance off Arnold. The opening stand of 24 was Australia's second-highest of the series and the best since the first innings at Old Trafford, but when John Snow upped his pace and uprooted Stackpole's off stump at 2 for 34, it was familiar terrain for the Chappell brothers.

Greg Chappell responded by thumping the first ball he received from Snow (a full toss) down the ground for four, and Ian followed by clipping Arnold wide of mid-wicket before producing a spanking cover drive to the fence. The Chappells put on 44 in 47 minutes before Snow complained about the shape of the ball. A new ball was produced and rubbed into the bowler's footmarks before being tossed to Illingworth for inspection. Fast bowlers' claims that machinery-made modern balls were inferior to hand-made balls were commonplace. Cricket ball manufacturers emphasised that the materials used to create the ball (cork and leather) remained the same. Ian Chappell hooked in front and behind square leg while Greg stood upright and drove confidently.

By half past two, the Chappells had handled four different seam bowlers with aplomb. After 32 overs, Underwood bowled for the first time. Greg Chappell played a maiden to Underwood while Ian dispatched the first two balls from Illingworth to the boundary, initially with a drive through the covers and then a sweep to deep fine leg. Greg Chappell brought up Australia's 100 in just over two hours and, as the afternoon progressed, the younger Chappell displayed a greater sense of certainty at the crease.

Ian Chappell played for turn when there was no turn, edging Underwood to Parfitt at slip, who moved the wrong way and spilled the chance. Just before tea, Greg made his first error with an inside edge off Arnold that narrowly missed leg stump hurtling to the boundary.

A growing sense of momentum and canny running between the wickets helped the Chappells reach a double-century stand, the first between brothers in Test cricket, as shadows encroached The Oval's surface. When Greg, on 113, tried to drive Illingworth to the boundary for the second time in successive balls he was beaten by flight and lobbed a gentle catch to Tony Greig at midwicket. Swishing his bat in disgust as he left the crease, Greg had calmed by the time he approached the crowd of 28,000 standing as he walked into the Members' Pavilion.

In the middle, Ian Chappell, with arms folded, watched proudly as his brother disappeared into the sea of faces. The Australian captain knew he largely played the sheet anchor role while Greg batted with ease. If any more evidence was needed that Greg Chappell was a world-class batsman, his innings century at The Oval had confirmed it. Chappell's on side was marked by standing up straight, driving and flicking the ball off his hip (between the square leg and the bowler), contributing three-quarters of his runs.

By the close of play, Australia, with three wickets down, was just ten runs behind England's total. Ian Chappell was undefeated on 107, reaching his century with an edge. Adding to the occasion of the second day's play for the Chappells, their parents Martin and Jeanne and brother, Trevor, watched on from the stands. Ian saw the day as a reward for 'all the work they had done and all the things they had given up to help us'.

After play, Martin Chappell, who had filmed some of his sons' innings, walked around The Oval outfield where they had made history. Ray Lindwall in the *Sun* predicted that Greg Chappell would soon become a great of the game. 'I'd put only Sobers, Boycott, Richards and Clive Lloyd ahead of him, with Barlow and Stackpole just about on a par.' Richie Benaud praised Ian, believing it to be the Australian captain's greatest hour. 'Ian Chappell will play many better innings for Australia in years to come. He will make many more runs than yesterday at The Oval, but he will never play a more valuable innings for his side.' Benaud also rated Greg Chappell's hundred the equal of his first innings century at Lord's.

John Snow started day three with two intimidating bouncers at Ian Chappell, who replied with a square cut and off-drive for successive boundaries. Snow stood on the pitch, hands on hips, before taking off his jumper and rolling up his sleeves. Snow's stare at the batsman remained, but much had changed since the previous Ashes series. Ross Edwards flicked at Snow and was taken low on the leg side by Knott, who was too busy catching the ball to appeal. Snow pleaded to the umpire, and Edwards looked like he was ready to walk, but umpire Fagg remained unmoved. On 118, Ian Chappell top-edged Arnold to Snow at deep fine leg, who moved in four paces from the boundary to take the catch. Chappell's first Test century in England consumed 331 minutes but included 20 boundaries. It was the classic definition of a captain's knock. Underwood then deceived Sheahan, who was caught bat-pad at a silly point, and Marsh was bowled for a duck leaving Australia, 6 for 310.

Edwards, with his upright running and neat, brisk steps, now held the Australian batting together with John Inverarity. At tea, WACA executive Bert Drew joined the thousands of fans strolling the outfield, impressed by the flint-like surface. Numerous impromptu cricket games sprung up as Drew wondered whether it might be a useful tactic to use at the WACA to encourage youngsters.

Extended light rain delayed play before Illingworth brought Underwood on from the Vauxhall End and Snow from the opposite (Pavilion) end. Underwood bowled Edwards for 79, ending a knock of deft cuts and elegant drives. Inverarity's cautious 28 closed when he skied a catch from Underwood to Greig. Thirty-seven minutes before stumps, the Australians successfully appealed against the light, leading by 110 runs with two wickets in hand.

In late summer sunlight, Paul Sheahan joined Keith Stackpole for a meal. Sheahan again had been dismissed cheaply by Underwood, and doubt lingered. Stackpole remained upbeat, convincing Sheahan to play his natural attacking game. 'You can have self-doubt, yet it doesn't appear like that to the outside world. What matters is the little voice in the back of your head. I often wondered whether I was good enough and tough enough to play at that level,' Sheahan recalled. What was certain was that Sheahan needed to score runs in the second innings.

When Edrich and Wood opened England's innings, they trailed by 115 runs. By lunch, they had made it to 56 without loss. At first slip, Ian Chappell grimaced when Wood, on one, flashed at Massie, and the ball flew shoulder-high to Greg Chappell, who spilled the chance. Lillee moved one ball so sharply outside off stump that it passed Wood and Rod Marsh, with Ian Chappell at slip injuring his shoulder diving to make the save. Edrich was bowled by Lillee immediately after lunch without adding to the score, and Parfitt fell to the same bowler. The departing batsmen had each scored 18. The dismissal marked the last time the jaunty Parfitt played for England.

Wood reached 50 from 113 balls, and in the next over John Hampshire hit successive boundaries off Mallett, the first elegantly through extra cover, the second a crude shot through mid-on. Umpire Rhodes warned Mallett for the second time for running on the pitch before he bowled around the wicket. Watson had Hampshire caught high in the slips by Ian Chappell, the ball and fieldsman moving in what looked like synchronised movement.

D'Oliveira batted so carefully that he added just one of the 17 runs scored in partnership with Wood before tea. Forty runs from six overs after tea, with 22 struck off Lillee, signalled a change in approach.

Inverarity was brought on to bowl. D'Oliveira was dropped by Marsh and then, in combination with Wood, scored at a run a minute. Just when a Test century on debut seemed within reach, a Massie inswinger caught Wood in front lbw for 90, ending four hours and 35 minutes at the crease. D'Oliveira's valuable knock of 43, which took the score to 5 for 205, closed when he edged a low chance to Ian Chappell at first slip. Illingworth, who had spent Sunday in bed with tonsillitis and faced a golden pair, began with a drive to the extra cover boundary and survived the 45 minutes until stumps with Greig to take the score to 5 for 227.

The first over of day five, bowled by Mallett, conceded 13 runs – four extras and nine to Illingworth. Just before midday, with the new ball taken, Greig struck Lillee for four boundaries. Two flashed past point, the others through square leg. The next over, the England captain cut and glanced Massie, taking the boundary toll to six in nine deliveries.

Marsh took Greig's attempted cut on the second attempt off Lillee, while Knott was dropped by Stackpole the next ball. Lillee captured his 30th wicket of the series when Illingworth, on 31, played across the line to a full-pitch ball. Knott cut and drove Lillee, Massie and Watson to the ropes, while Snow deftly glanced and pushed before being caught at slip by Stackpole off a straight ball from Mallett. Arnold kept Knott company, who reached his 50 with a leg-side push off Lillee in the over before lunch.

England's innings ended when Knott's middle stump was upended by Lillee on 63, scored in just over two hours. With England bowled out for 356 off 121 overs, Australia needed 242 runs to win the Test and draw the series with more than a day and a half to spare.

Australia had scored 252 (chasing 342) on a seaming Old Trafford pitch, so their chance to level the series sat tantalisingly close. However, Ian Chappell was barely settled in the dressing room when Watson was lbw to Arnold for 6. So early were his arrivals at the crease that Ian Chappell had become a de facto opener. Stackpole attacked, lightening the mood in the dressing room and showing what could be done. An hour before stumps, Illingworth twisted his ankle, causing the loss of a handy off spinner and astute leader at a crucial point in the game. At the close, Australia was 1 for 116. Stackpole was riding his luck undefeated on 70 after earlier driving at Greig and top edging to slip where Parfitt could only reach the ball but couldn't stop it from going to the boundary. It was the tenth time the Australian opener had been dropped during the series.

Day six and Ian Chappell was driven to the ground in a £30,000 Aston Martin (owned by his employer WD & HO Wills). As he watched the long lines of spectators waiting to get into The Oval, he thought about how crucial the first sessions had become that summer. Chappell asked the English driver, who had never seen a game of cricket before, what he thought of the game.

'I love it', was the response. Well, Chappell thought to himself, if this bloke likes it, we must be doing something right. The casual conversation also helped Chappell switch on for the day. Chappell knew the Ashes battles had been reinvigorated. And it wasn't just English fans. Capitalising on the interest, the ABC announced it would telecast the final day's play via live BBC satellite stream for the first time. The move represented a significant shift for Australian sporting fans and more evidence that the national broadcaster was visionary in its approach. Real-time replays had already been introduced in 1970/71 with slow motion replays, close-up shots, and cameras square of the wicket soon to follow in 1973/74.

On the final morning, the camera panned to The Oval's gasometer before narrowing to the tall blond figure of Tony Greig, who was measuring his run-up. Fifteen thousand kilometres away, Australian cricket fans settled in to watch the sights and the sounds of the Oval crowd as a large West Indian contingent banged on drums and blew whistles. Added to Illingworth's injury were John Snow's bruised arm and D'Oliveira's strained back muscle. When John Hampshire dropped Stackpole at slip from the first ball he faced for the day, England's players' shoulders slumped; however, after Stackpole (79) edged to Knott, Ian Chappell (37) and Edwards (1) soon followed, Australia looked like losing its nerve with three wickets falling for five runs. The Australian captain's dismissal was dramatic as he swept Underwood and top-edged the ball into his jaw (before being caught in short by substitute Bob Willis at silly mid-on).

The Australian dressing room sat anxiously watching Greg Chappell and Paul Sheahan as they eased the tourists closer to the target. Underwood made a ball jump almost vertically to strike Greg Chappell in the throat, and when he was lbw for 16, with Australia 5 for 171, there was plenty of work to do. Marsh was soon beaten three times outside off stump by Greig before Sheahan helped counter the pressure. The pair began by taking Underwood for five runs in six balls before Marsh slog-swept Underwood over the square-leg boundary. With the wicket slow, turning and often unpredictable, Sheahan made a decision. 'I thought, right, Derek, it's either you or me, old boy.' He decided to sweep whatever ball came next and leave the result to fate. Sheahan hit the ball flush in the middle of the bat to the Archbishop Tenison's School side boundary. Underwood raised his eyebrows in surprise, and Sheahan knew he had won the battle.

With the arrival of the new ball, acting captain Edrich used Greig, Arnold, Snow and Underwood in near consecutive overs without success. Sheahan's orthodox stability and Marsh's aggressive gumption had steadied Australia. With Australia needing four runs to win, a loyal group of West Indian supporters moved to the boundary line. One picked up a flag and waved it around his head, impersonating Muhammad Ali with cries of 'We are the greatest'.

During the 1970s, England Test grounds reverberated with thousands of British Afro-Caribbeans gleefully celebrating the opposition sides' victories. Fans banged on tin cans beating rhythms. Cricket became a rallying point to promote Caribbean independence, which was emerging from major political and social upheaval. It became important to watch England defeated, even if it was not by a West Indian side. In 1960, just three West Indian nations had achieved independence from European colonies; by the early 1980s, it had grown to 16. As former West Indian paceman Colin Croft put it,

'West Indians [who] had been born in colonial times but grew up in independent times . . . started thinking like West Indians and not like Englishmen living in the West Indies'. The West Indian fans were well and truly behind Australia that summer.

Marsh hit the winning runs 39 minutes after lunch. Their unbeaten stand of 71 in 87 minutes gave Australia a five-wicket win, drawing the series 2-all. Marsh and Sheahan wore grins from ear to ear as they waved their bats and ran from the ground. Sheahan was undefeated on 44 in 140 minutes. Marsh's 43 had featured five boundaries, including three off four balls from Underwood's last over (Marsh had taken just 51 balls while Sheahan was more sedate consuming 121 deliveries). When Marsh entered the Australian dressing room he fell over and was supported by teammates. Champagne corks were popped and Foster beers opened as Australia celebrated. Ian Chappell, who had joined the BBC television broadcast a few minutes before the game ended, had by now rushed back to the rooms. On air, Chappell had just thanked his junior cricket coach Lynn Fuller, who mentored him and Greg during their formative years. In Adelaide, early in the morning of 17 August, Fuller was sitting on his couch watching. Ian Chappell's words so moved Fuller that he later wrote thanking him. Former England captain (and recently critical) Ted Dexter even dropped into the Australian dressing room, after collecting $400 from the Chappells' centuries at The Oval with $10 each-way bet at the odds of 10 to 1.

The TCCB also had cause for celebration, with 370,000 spectators paying a world record of half-a-million dollars (Australian) to watch the series. The West Indian portion of the crowd stood beneath The Oval balcony accepting the bottles of champagne lowered by the celebrating Australians. Rod Marsh jumped onto the table of the Australian dressing room table and sang the team's victory song, 'A sprig of wattle in my hand . . . Australia, you fucking beauty'. The song, inspired by Henry Lawson's 1887 poem 'Flag of the Southern Cross', was picked up by Ian Chappell in his Lancashire League playing days. Chappell watched on, nursing a cold can of South Australian Southwark bitter, looking like a street fighter in his pale-green-and-gold tracksuit and a bloody scrape on the jaw. Chappell didn't mind the pain, remarking, 'I won't feel a thing tonight.' He knew that Australia could now defeat anyone.

English newspaper headlines were fulsome in their praise for the young Australian side. 'You've earned it Aussies' headlined *The Express*. 'The Australians reap the reward of youth', wrote the *Guardian*, while the *Daily Mirror* described the tourists 'The graduates – Aussies pass the final test the hard way'. John Arlott wrote, 'There have been many other rubbers in which more great players took part, but few indeed have ever been so even, fluctuating, exciting, full of character, played in better spirit or with greater enjoyment'.

The difference between the sides statistically rested with the strength of the Australian top order; four had averaged over 45 while no Englishman reached 40. Lillee and Massie shared the wicket-taking spoils with 54 wickets between them, better than any three English bowlers on aggregate, and all but one (Underwood) on average. England won on the two wickets favouring bowlers; Australia won on the more even wickets and had the better of the draw at Trent Bridge. What was clear was that Australia was in ascendancy and England was on the wane. By the end of the series, Lillee had taken 31 wickets, ten of them caught by Marsh

It was time for the Australian players to celebrate, and the wives who visited for the last three weeks of the tour (although they had to stay at different hotels). Lyndall Edwards, Nancy Massie, Jane Inverarity, Roslyn Marsh, Caroline Walters and Jane Sheahan were snapped by the press strolling hand in hand across the ground during the final Test. Marsh recalled how Ros, a schoolteacher, had to work as a waitress in the evenings to pay for her airfare to England, tasks she managed with a new baby and the help of her parents.

Soon rumblings began in the English press about the home side's performance. An MCC team chosen to tour India, Pakistan and Ceylon included only five of the side that played in the Sixth Test (Geoff Arnold, Tony Greig, Alan Knott, Derek Underwood and Barry Wood). Ray Illingworth, John Snow, Geoff Boycott, John Edrich, Mike Smith and Richard Hutton all made themselves unavailable, while Basil D'Oliveira and Brian Luckhurst missed selection.

Chapter Twelve

Winding down slowly

The tour, now well into its sixth month, was starting to drag. Sheahan knew the loneliness of a long tour and a lack of Test cricket from his time under Lawry in 1968. 'To play and win Test matches is what you go away for. You want to be at the top of the tree, and if you're not, you try and do your bit for the team, but it's not quite the same.' Jeff Hammond found life very difficult as the youngest tourist.

> A long tour without playing Test cricket could be lonely, although there was great camaraderie. I missed my mentors. Terry Jenner wasn't there, and Ian Chappell had 16 other blokes to look after, including me. I hadn't quite grown up and wasn't as life-smart. I doubt I had the maturity of a 20 or 21-year-old. I matured later when I was out of Test cricket, I had to mature very quickly then.

The Australians were relaxed during the remaining eight matches of the tour (three first-class, three ODIs and two limited over). Playing Kent, Doug Walters had an overdue return to form, scoring 150, and Greg Chappell blazed an undefeated 141. Gleeson troubled the Kent batsmen and Jeff Hammond took four cheap wickets. Greg Chappell added five catches, securing a case of whiskey awarded for the best all-round performance.

Australia played England in three one-day games over the August Bank Holiday weekend, attracting 55,000 spectators and £46,000 in gate money. The 55-over 'one-day Tests', played at Manchester, Lord's and Birmingham, saw England take the series 2–1, the Prudential Trophy, and most (£2600) of the £4000 prizemoney.

England won the first ODI at Old Trafford by six wickets, revealing a greater experience in the shorter format. Australian eyebrows were raised when it was announced that the Leeds club (owners of Headingley) would be digging up the playing square and renewing the surface.

Before the second encounter at Lord's, Bob Massie was presented with the two balls with which he took his 16-wicket haul by MCC President Freddie Brown.

A crowd of 22,000 watched on in the late-afternoon sun as Australia prevailed, winning by five wickets with four overs to play. England triumphed in the third encounter by two wickets at Edgbaston in a close contest

The one-day matches revealed England's superior experience and Australia's ability to learn quickly how to approach the game's new format. Dennis Amiss became the first England player to score a century in international cricket that summer, and Geoff Boycott returned, scoring 25, 8 and 41. Arlott wrote that Boycott played Lillee bowling off a shortened run with 'a cool certainty', while Keith Stackpole thought Lillee (who also removed Boycott twice in the one-dayers) had dominated the England opener throughout the summer. Boycott had struggled in the Tests scoring 8, 47, 11 and 6, lacking the confidence he'd shown in Australia.

When the Australians lost their penultimate first-class match against Lancashire by nine wickets after two days of play, it was obvious the tour had gone on too long. Their second innings of 154 barely lasted two-and-a-half hours.

Fixtures against TN Pearce's Eleven at Scarborough provided a festival end. Graeme Watson found some late summer form with the bat striking 157 on the second day of the three-day match. In Australia's second innings, Greg Chappell, batting at number seven, helped himself to 67 runs in 22 minutes.

The matches after the Fifth Test reinforced Ian Chappell's belief that tours needed to be shorter.

Long it was but certainly memorable and so vastly different from today's pyrotechnic visits chock full of different formats of the game. Lillee recalled Mick Jagger visiting the Australians at The Oval with his dad Joe, who was a member of Surrey. 'Jagger told me he was hooked on the game and watching me bowl reminded him of the ballet. I'm not sure what Mick had been drinking but I don't think it was Evian.' Mallett described the tour as 'the best of them all in our era'.

> We played good cricket against Ray Illingworth's England team, drank half pints of Double Diamond lager with Mick Jagger in the front bar of the Waldorf hotel in the Aldwych most nights when the team was at its London HQ, rubbed shoulders with actors, comedians, singers and cut two records for Penny Farthing Records.

Leadership on tour

Ian Chappell had proved an innovative Australian captain in the circumstances, willing to lead from the front, fiercely loyal to his side, a motivator when the tour became tough, a great ambassador for his country, and an astute captain. Chappell's success was no accident, he had worked hard for it. Dennis Lillee knew this when they ran together. Lillee expected to burn Chappell off on the eight-kilometre round trip through London streets, but when they returned to the Waldorf Hotel Ian Chappell was just a few steps behind.

Although Ian Chappell was still emerging as a Test captain; he had been able to turn a team that was on its knees into a winning formula once again. The *Evening Standard*'s John Thicknesse observed, 'Tactically, he has a lot to learn – what young captain doesn't?' There was little doubt that Chappell had made a first-class impression on and off the field, and was adept at public relations. Benaud sang Chappell's praises. 'It took him a while to get settled, but that's normal for a captain on a tour of England. He was very careful with his players and got on well with everyone. I was very impressed.' Mallett thought that the main reason that 1972 was seen as such a defining tour was because it heralded the emergence of Ian Chappell as a leader of standing.

Chappell had shown that he was a leader who led by example, having to walk into bat on most occasions during the Test series when Australia was under pressure. He would also field in close in the most dangerous position when required. Chappell could inject enthusiasm into the players when England was on top in matches and refused to lose faith in his side. He picked the side up after they lost at Old Trafford and then again at Leeds.

Chappell was a quick learner and knew who to learn from. He carefully observed the ever-calm Illingworth. 'There are times as a captain when you had to back off. There's a good player at the crease, and he's playing well, and you've got to pull back a little. Illy never pulled back to the point where, as a batsman, you thought he was not trying to get me out, that he was just trying to restrict my scoring. He always lets you know he's trying to get you out.'

Importantly, Chappell recognised the importance of a good working relationship between captain and manager. Ray Steele was an urbane disciplinarian with an ability to solve even the most complex problems diplomatically with a charismatic style. His ability to handle off-field matters was critical in allowing the captain to concentrate on team performance. Steele, although in his 50s, brought a fresh approach to the game and was popular universally among the players. David Colley thought Steele was an extraordinary character.

> He was tough, had a nickname 'Castor' as in 'Cast of Steel' but he understood the game and understood sportsmen, understood the media. He was just the coolest cat and kept reminding us that our job was to keep focused . . . you had 17 individuals with different styles of people, and he'd worked every one of us out. If we got off

> the straight and narrow he'd quickly pull us into line. He was one of the greatest human beings I'd met in my life . . . the consummate politician and ultimate knockabout who was a rogue but a tough and demanding rogue. We all got some discipline when required.

Players knew that if they were called to Steele's room they were in trouble. Steele was a stickler for doing the right thing if a commitment was made. Colley learned this firsthand when some of the team were asked to play golf at Sunningdale and Greg Chappell pulled out late in the evening the day before. Colley agreed to take his place but slept through an early morning call, took a cab to Sunningdale, and paid out of his own money to play nine holes and provide entertainment for the guests. When he returned to the hotel Colley found himself called into Steele's room and given a hefty fine because he hadn't fulfilled his obligations. 'It turned out to be a very expensive day and I played lousy golf.'

But was Steele, as a manager, everything he was made out to be by the players? Only a few years later, during the Packer era, Australian players complained about his lack of player management and communication as they took on close to full-strength opposition sides with little or no administrative support. Also, Steele was one of the Australian administrators decrying Kerry Packer's takeover of world cricket and the financial rewards for players that came with it – the very reason World Series Cricket came about.

The 1972 Ashes tour, much like the 1948 Invincibles in England and the West Indies in Australia in 1961, was a pivotal moment in cricket history. With its unrestricted television coverage and record-breaking attendances at some Tests, the tour saw interest in Test cricket in the UK higher than for decades. This surge of interest also spread to Australia, with numbers at grade practices across the country and bat sales at their highest since 1960.

While Ian Chappell took time to settle and learn the tactics of captaining, he left English shores with a reputation for inspiring his players and sound tactical judgment.

Australia, though, was on a slow and, at times, troubled path to the top of world cricket. When asked about the world's Test nations in order of superiority, Ray Steele ranked Australia third and England fourth (after South Africa and India). While Australia had drawn the away series, it experienced its first Test victory since it defeated India at Madras in 1969, and its first Aussie win against England since 1968. The promising victories in England instilled a sense of optimism about the future of Australian cricket.

Chapter Thirteen

Legacy

Despite the tour's success, questions were raised about the Australians' behaviour. Had the Australians' hard-nosed approach occasionally spilled over to something unacceptable? There had been banter during the Test series, but general respect between the sides.

Ian Chappell's side would later be described as the 'Ugly Australians', a tag Chappell had always strongly rebutted, describing abuse as 'mindless rubbish'. Lillee would snarl at batsmen, but so too would Snow. There were a few send offs to batsmen, and boorish ripostes, but barely enough to believe that Chappell's Australians were much different to any other Australian sides.

Years later when speaking to journalist Frank Crook, Ross Edwards remembered a couple of instances of the Australians sledging in county games but not in the Test matches. Richie Benaud saw it as ruthless efficiency, writing 'Ian Chappell was quite likely to trample them [England] into the ground with his long spikes, offer a calm "sorry about that, pal", and then get on with the task of winning another match for Australia – in keeping with his magnificent performance on this tour'. Egyptian-born Oxford University and Surrey player turned journalist E.M. Wellings was more forthright in his views in the *Daily Mirror*, believing umpires were subject to bullying from the Australians.

> Too many batsmen have been shouted at by the touring players this summer, even in Test cricket . . . This side had been building

> an unenviable reputation as the worst behaved in memory. More and more reports come about their behaviour on the field, of their bad language and their habit of trying to talk their opponents out.

Wellings cited 'unpleasant' behaviour, with young Hampshire batsman David Turner, having scored a century, sent on his way with a fingers-up gesture, just as West Indian Keith Boyce playing for Essex received a month later. Another example was an 'Australian player stripped to their waist' on the Lord's players balcony when the tourists played Middlesex. 'Our visitors should not confuse the pavilion at Lord's with the beach at Bondi', said Wellings. Wellings was somewhat of a contrarian and perhaps more tellingly noted the Australian bowlers slowed the over rate down to 80 balls an hour at times and followed through on and close to the line of the wicket. Yet the umpires pulled up any Australian bowlers running on the wicket, and the slow over rate was one of the challenges with Dennis Lillee running in from 40 metres.

During a county match against Northamptonshire, *People*, a mass-circulation tabloid, featured the headline 'Rude Aussies are Rapped'. The Australians were described by some staff at the nearby county tavern as 'disgusting, ignorant and rude'. Waitress Kath Whatt was the main critic, in what sounds like a Monty Python skit: 'Nothing I could do was right . . . One of the players kept going to the private server and helping himself to the cheese and biscuits.' The hotel manager, Mrs Ray Bird, joined the chorus of dissatisfaction, saying she'd seen the same player do his 'cheese and biscuit routine' at lunch on the third day. When Mrs Bird told the player that he had 'no right to do that', she was showered with a handful of biscuits and 'Keep your bloody cheese'. The Australians were also accused of being impertinent when they could only get peaches and not bananas for dessert. Northamptonshire secretary Ken Turner immediately defended the Australians. 'I was there at lunch for all three days. I saw nothing of this alleged behaviour.' Ray Steele concurred, having 'seen nothing of the reported incidents'.

Benaud, who travelled with the Australians throughout the tour, was eager to hose down any speculation:

> No, I thought it was one of the best Australian sides I have ever seen away . . . for the record I rang the managers of the 22 hotels at which the Australians stayed in England and asked as a journalist for their comment on the Australian behaviour. All 22 reported back that they would be glad to have the Australians back.

There was little doubt that Benaud was a great supporter of Chappell's side and also came from an era where little, if any, off-field controversies were made public (unless the police reported it).

Perhaps it was just the tourists' sense of arrogance that was building among a team that would later demolish sides with confidence and aggression, aided by Jeff Thomson's firepower.

Would it be surprising if the Australians, at times, became somewhat tetchy? They toured England from 17 April to 30 September, some five-and-a-half months. By the end they were exhausted. After five Test matches, 25 first class and 11 non-first-class matches, the players were finally making their way home. Ray Steele noted that Australia's tour of 14 wins and ten draws from 35 matches justified the selectors sending a younger party. Seen to be more progressive than most administrators, Steele intended recommending shorter tours.

The standard of Australian fielding was as high as it ever had been. Ian Chappell's side also featured a starburst of world-class talent in Dennis Lillee, Rod Marsh and the Chappells. Lillee was now the fastest and most exciting pace bowler seen in England since Wes Hall. Greg Chappell was among the top batsmen in the world. Rod Marsh was a highly efficient keeper to spin and pace as well as being rambunctious with the bat. He was also an astute reader of the game, and ever willing to pass on information standing next to Ian Chappell at first slip. Australia would conquer all before them for the next four years. Following the 1972 tour, they defeated Pakistan, New Zealand, the West Indies and England. When Greg Chappell took over in 1975/76 (with Ian still playing) they crushed the West Indies in what was referred to as 'the world championship of cricket'.

Where are they now?

In the years that followed, members of the 1972 Australian team had fluctuating fortunes. Within a year of his triumph at the Lord's Test, Bob Massie's international career was over. When South Australia played Western Australia at the WACA during the 1972/73 season Ian Chappell was able to negotiate Massie more easily than previously. The early indication of decline proved well founded.

Massie's 1973 tour to the West Indies was ill-fated. Feeling sick on the long flight to the Caribbean, Massie was hospitalised in Jamaica for five days on arrival. Underdone he played at Montego Bay against the President's Eleven and struggled. 'The ball was shredded in 10 overs. I'd rarely played in conditions where I couldn't swing it. Eventually I tried to cut the ball off the wicket, which was fraught for me as it messed up my action. I didn't have the same control.'

Massie also realised that playing cricket all year round for four-and-a-half years without a break had taken a heavy toll on him. His desire to play at the top level remained, but he found it difficult to bowl consistently well.

Massie spent a year trying to regain form but knew the state selectors were looking elsewhere when he wasn't asked to bowl in the second innings against South Australia at Adelaide Oval in 1974/75. 'I rang Alan Edwards [WA chair of selectors] and told him that's enough for me. I won't be training with the state squad any more. You know where to find me if you need me.' It was a significant moment for Massie, who had been in the WA squad since 1964/65. He missed the camaraderie of the dressing room but stayed in touch with old teammates, 'where we remembered the fun we had playing and didn't really speak about the matches'. Massie's exit from first-class cricket prompted a shift into coaching and media roles. Through former teammate Ian Brayshaw's connections, Massie began a career commentating Sheffield Shield cricket on the ABC that lasted 22 years, including a highlight of working with Alan McGilvray in a Test match. Post retirement in his mid-50s he coached at private schools in Perth.

There were many theories as to why Massie's career fell away so dramatically.

Try as he might Massie struggled to match his fitness in the lead up to the English tour. Never an athlete Massie easily put on weight. Whereas some players went to a restaurant to eat steak or fish Massie would enjoy a pie from the corner store. Inverarity, who captained Massie for WA, thought Massie 'had got the yips like a golfer'. Perhaps Keith Stackpole was right when he noted that highly successful debuts can put overwhelming pressure on players. Whatever the reasons behind Massie's lack of continued success his feats forever remain etched in cricketing history.

Greg Chappell, after his two peerless tons, the first at Lord's and the second at The Oval, was on his way to becoming one of the best batsmen in the world. Chappell had learned to set a task and not be satisfied until it was completed.

His ascendancy as a batsman was rapid. It had only been four years earlier that Sir Donald Bradman had advised a change in his grip, all dispensed while playing a shadow drive where the bat was moved so fast it 'looked like a propeller'. Bradman, then 59, played the shadow shot twice before saying, 'This was my grip, and it served me OK.' Greg Chappell took off to the nets and immediately started hitting the ball with greater regularity and strength through the off side.

By the end of the 1974/75 Ashes summer, Greg Chappell had dominated, scoring 608 at an average of 55.27. The following summer, as captain against the West Indies, he managed 702 runs at 117. He became an integral part of World Series Cricket and continued to lead Australia at home, eventually retiring from Test cricket at the end of the 1983/84 summer, finishing as he had started it, with a ton. His Test career average of 53.86 revealed an ability against all types of bowlers in all conditions that marked him as one of the greatest batsmen Australia has produced. Greg Chappell later coached South Australia, and India, was Cricket Australia's national talent manager and selector, and commentated for Channel Nine and the ABC.

John Inverarity would never tour England again as an Australian cricketer. His two tours represented some success but revealed a player not quite Test class as a batsman or bowler. Ironically, Inverarity's selection in 1968 paved the way for Greg Chappell to play for Somerset, providing the younger Chappell with invaluable experience in English conditions. Inverarity's main contribution to Australian cricket came after 1972, when he became a significant leader in the domestic game, playing 223 matches and scoring 11,777 runs. Inverarity's career needs to be viewed through the prism of how he saw himself as a teacher first and a cricketer second. Having taught at Tonbridge he coached Kent and Warwickshire and later worked as Warden of St George's College (made up of largely rural WA students). Inverarity was also the Australian Chairman of Selectors for two-and-a-half years and a member of the University of Western Australia's Senate and the Board of Governors.

For David Colley, the back injuries that plagued the second half of his 1972 tour continued. Back home he underwent surgery to repair three spinal fractures. Colley's three Ashes Tests are a reminder of a brief but eventful spell at the top. 'It's only when you get older you realise how important an Ashes tour is. Every day you were walking in heaven. You were considered an important person.'

Despite his injuries, Colley's first-class career spanned 87 games taking 236 wickets at 31.60. By the time he retired, he also had 527 grade wickets at 19.65 to his name. He ended a 20-year district career on a high, winning the O'Reilly Medal as the best and fairest in Sydney grade cricket in 1983. By the age of 75 he'd had two knee replacements, two back operations and a triple by-pass (after a heart attack in England).

John Gleeson played his final Test in England in 1972. His 29-Test career encompassed four years (1967/68 to 1972), including tours to India and South Africa. Gleeson toured South Africa with Derek Robins' team in 1973/74 and played a final first-class season with Western Province. He finished with 93 Test and 430 first-class wickets. He later served on the first governing committee of Kerry Packer's World Series Cricket. Having worked 40 years for Telecom, Gleeson died in Tamworth in October 2016 at the age of 78.

After the tour, Jeff Hammond picked up work as a PMG technician and began engineering studies. Despite not playing a Test in England, Hammond knew his cricket stocks had risen, and he'd become a 'smarter bowler'. 'I would listen to advice, decipher and analyse to the nth degree.' Hammond cut down on his smoking and added muscle bulk by working out at the gym following advice from Ian Chappell that he needed to get stronger.

For Hammond, the fruits of the 1972 England tour were born when Australia toured the West Indies in 1973. Suddenly, with Lillee injured and Massie ineffective, Hammond's fast-medium swingers were in high demand as he played all five Tests, picking up 15 wickets at 32. Ian Chappell believes Hammond wouldn't have been able to achieve this without the experience of the 1972 England tour, remembering, 'A lot of people thought that "Bomber" was a dumb bastard but he was far from it. He was particularly smart as a fast bowler and learned from watching and observing things that players like Lillee and others did.' Hammond's smarts were on show during the First Test at Kingston.

On the third day, with Alvin Kallicharran and Lawrence Rowe having taken the total beyond 150 on a very flat track, Hammond told Chappell he wanted to bounce Kallicharran. 'You've got two balls to get him out,' Ian Chappell responded. 'But I'm glad you told me so I can give you some protection.' The next ball Kallicharran was caught by Marsh from a Hammond bouncer.

The West Indies tour proved a windfall for both Jeff Hammond and Max Walker, each learning from the other on long beach walks. Hammond's workload in Australia's 2–0 series win, however, was a cause of back problems that plagued him for two seasons. The 1975/76 summer started promisingly when Hammond took 4 for 58 against the visiting West Indies but, later that season, he required back surgery. Hammond eventually reinvented himself as a batsman, one season winning the batting average and aggregate for Prospect. He started bowling again after acupuncture treatment proved successful but never recaptured his earlier pace. He returned to first-class cricket as an allrounder and was appointed South Australian coach in the early 1990s. Hammond coached South Australia to a Sheffield Shield win after the famous drawn final against Western Australia in 1995/96 and coaching jobs in South Africa and England followed.

By anyone's standards, Rod Marsh in 1972 enjoyed a summer to remember. By summer's close, several English counties were touting his services, with Sussex, Surrey, Middlesex and Essex making approaches. Marsh had started the template of Australian keepers who could also hold their place as a batsman. Ian Chappell also remembered how valuable Marsh was as a tactician. Marsh views the tour as a time he 'became a hell of a lot better at the game . . . it was a tour to remember'. The boy whose mum had wanted her son to become a concert pianist instead became one of the most decorated wicketkeepers in the history of the game, and was once a world record holder for most Test dismissals and the first Australian keeper to score a Test century.

Marsh became emblematic of Chappell's brigade of tough men, yet there was an inherent sense of fairness and goodwill in his play. Greg Chappell described Marsh 'as the spiritual leader of the group'. Marsh's combative walk, chest hair sprouting from an unbuttoned shirt, drooping moustache, neat yet sprawling keeping style, tight one-day shirts, and take-no-prisoners style of play helped define Australian cricket during the 1970s. He played hard on the field but was always scrupulously fair. Along with Shane Warne he was probably the best Test captain that Australia never had.

Marsh's formidable career spanned 257 first-class matches, scoring 11,067 runs and completing 869 dismissals. He played 96 Test matches and, fittingly, his 355 dismissals were the same as Dennis Lillee's final tally. Marsh remembered his relationship with Lillee.

> I've played with him so much now that most of the time, I know what he is going to do before he has bowled. I know from the way he runs up, the angle, the speed, where he hits the crease – where the ball is going to be. I can see the way his mind is working and I can virtually bowl his over for him, ball by ball.

Marsh's drinking prowess was also renowned and set in cricketing folklore when he broke Doug Walters' 44-can beer-drinking record.

Marsh retired along with Greg Chappell and Dennis Lillee at the end of the 1983/84 season after the disappointment of continually being ignored as a possible Australian captain. He was installed as the coach and later cricket director at the Australian Cricket Academy in 1991, four years after it was formed, guiding players such as Ricky Pointing and Glenn McGrath. He also helped set up the ICC's coaching academy in Dubai and later took over England's academy before becoming an England selector. Poached by the ECB from 2001 his work contributed to England's unlikely 2005 Ashes win. He was later Cricket Australia's elite coaching development manager, as well as Chairman of the Australian Test selection panel for two years. He died in 2022, a week after having a heart attack in Bundaberg.

Keith Stackpole's only England tour saw success in all five Ashes Tests, scoring 114 in the first innings in Trent Bridge's Third test as well as passing 50 on five other occasions and averaging 53 for the series. Luck was on his side, but his aggressive approach helped take on the England attack from the first ball. Stackpole toured the West Indies with success in 1973, averaging 47 in four Tests, yet a year later, his

Test career was over. With scores of 10, 27, 4 and 9 against a mediocre New Zealand attack, Stackpole knew the end was near. Back injuries had limited his freedom of movement. 'I knew it would be my last Test against New Zealand at Eden Park but little did I know I'd get a pair. For a few years, the ball had looked the size of a basketball, and now it was looking more like the eye of a needle.' In the first innings, Stackpole lost sight of Richard Hadlee's first ball over the top of the sightscreen, tried to pull away from a head-high full toss, and helplessly watched on as the ball flicked the end of the bat and flew to Parker at first slip. His second innings ended with him fending off a Dick Collinge bouncer to Bevan Congdon at short leg for his second duck of the match. He finished his district career as captain-coach of Carlton, winning the Victorian Cricket Association Jack Ryder Medal in 1976, 1978 and 1979. He later became a commentator on Channel Nine and ABC radio while continuing his professional career with Rothmans.

When Stackpole retired from first-class cricket he had played 43 Tests and 167 first-class matches. Amazingly, as Stackpole revealed in his 1974 book *Not Just for Openers*, he played his entire career blind in his left eye and adapted using a open stance. He kept his disability secret for most of his career. Keith Stackpole died on 22 April 2025, aged 84.

Doug Walters failed against high-class seam bowling in Test matches in England despite touring four times. On the 1972 tour, Doug Walters' Test form was so poor that some critics thought he was finished as a Test player, but vice-captain Keith Stackpole was sympathetic. 'The pitches did more than the modern day largely because of the lack of the covering of the wicket during playing hours. I know Doug felt that some of his innings against county sides that summer were as good as any he had played.' After the tour Walters admitted that he found it hard.

> I think perhaps my style works against success . . . I've had trouble all the way through against the ball that seams off the soft English tracks. Yet if you find a good English wicket, there are few better surfaces on which to bat in the world.

While Walters' failures in England remained one of the mysteries of his career, Chappell recalled Walters not just as a great batsman but also as a highly astute cricketer in all ways. Ian Chappell remembered him as a tactician.

> He would stand deep in the covers and then give me this signal with his hands behind his back pretending he had a fox's tail. He was telling me that he was foxing the batsman by fielding so deep and that he would be able to stop a single or, even better still, run the batsman out.

He was also highly competitive and always thinking about how to get a wicket as a bowler and fieldsman. Despite his failures in England, Walters went on to play for Australia for close to another decade. He famously scored a ton in a session in Perth at the WACA against England in 1974/75 (one of three times he scored a Test century in a session) and later joined World Series Cricket. Walters' Test career ended in 1981 after a successful series against New Zealand. In 74 Tests he averaged 48.

When Paul Sheahan first toured England in 1968, he was just 21, tall, handsome and athletic. Adding to his flair was his smooth, efficient gliding movements in the covers. Perhaps it was Sheahan's pastime throwing stones at streetlights as a child that helped hone his skills, regardless he always found fielding fun. The two educators, Sheahan and John Inverarity, roomed together on the 1972 tour. It was, in many ways, a perfect match. They were both married with young children, shared similar tastes and, as Sheahan put it, 'the same idiotic sense of humour'. Sheahan's second innings at Leeds and The Oval at least proved he had converted some of the potential he promised under extreme pressure. His 31 Test match career ended in 1974 before his 28th birthday. Like Inverarity, he chose to become a professional teacher. Sheahan's Test career ended when he made himself unavailable for the 1974 tour of New Zealand (he had also been unavailable for the 1973 tour of the West Indies). He'd done so to take up a teaching position with Geelong Grammar. 'I had an opportunity I wanted to take and you couldn't really combine both . . . You don't play cricket for the rest of your life. I knew I had a limited time in the game.' Australian selector Sam Loxton had a robust response to Sheahan making himself unavailable, retorting, 'Well, that's the end of your Test career.'

Loxton's reaction was understandable. As a selector, he'd spent years trying to find Australia a strong opening pair and the Stackpole / Sheahan combination was going well. Sheahan later became the principal at his former school, Geelong College, and Melbourne Grammar, and worked in the media at ABC for ten years. One of the highlights was hosting *The Winners* (a VFL highlights show). A former president of the Melbourne Cricket Club, Sheahan retired at the age of 62 and now occupies his time with board appointments, most outside of the world of education.

Ashley Mallett went on to capture 138 wickets in 38 Tests, with his final appearance in 1980 at the Centenary Test. His bowling flourished under the leadership of Ian Chappell and he became a world-class gully fieldsman. He took 8 for 59 against Pakistan at Adelaide Oval in 1972/73 and played in his third Sheffield Shield-winning side in 1975/76. He eventually joined Kerry Packer's World Series Cricket, playing for the Cavaliers in country matches. He later worked as a spin bowling coach, commentator and writer. He showed a special interest in Indigenous cricketers and often visited Alice Springs for the national Indigenous cricket carnival. A great mentor to other writers (including this one), and author of 35 books, Mallett died of cancer at the age of 76 in 2021.

Ross Edwards, a player with a defensive style, saw his dream come true during the 1972 tour. He was well aware of his strengths and limitations, mainly playing square and off the pads. His patience was a key asset, believing 'if you let the ball go often enough you can get the bowlers to bowl where you want them to'.

Edwards toured the West Indies as the second keeper and played every match. Marsh kept in the Tests (that Edwards played as a batsman), but when he was rested for some of the Island games, Edwards had to play as keeper. By the time Edwards returned from the West Indies, he'd been playing for Australia for around 15 months and had 'ten dollars in the bank'. He was exhausted and broke. It was tough going for him and his young family. Edwards' accounting knowledge provided the background of two depositions to the Australian Board of Control regarding the need to increase player payments. It was ignored both times. By then the gloss of playing for Australia was starting to wear off.

Having to take time off to go on tour began to grate as he couldn't enjoy holidays with his family. 'Players started retiring because they couldn't afford to keep playing. From 1970 I didn't get a job for four years.' Edwards was part of the Australian annihilation of England, scoring 115 in the Second Test at Perth in 1974, and was at the other end when Doug Walters scored his century in a session with a six off the final ball of the day. He topped the Australian averages in the first men's World Cup before making 99 in the Lord's Test. After he retired from first-class cricket, Edwards played World Series Cricket, captaining the Cavaliers on their country tours, returning to Sheffield Shield cricket briefly to lead NSW. He later took on a Channel Nine executive's role in Sydney and other senior jobs with international broadcasters. A Ross Edwards stamp and coin commemorated the 50th anniversary of his undefeated 170 at Trent Bridge.

The 1972 tour for Graeme Watson was really one he shouldn't have made. He was still recovering from the horrendous head injury he suffered playing against the Rest of the World, and despite some success in county matches, he failed to replicate his form in the two Tests he played. Watson never represented Australia again and later moved to Sydney for work, becoming the first player to represent three states in the Sheffield Shield. Watson had great success at the domestic level, playing in four Sheffield Shield winning teams

(Victoria in 1966/67 and Western Australia in 1971/72, 1972/73 and 1974/75). He also joined World Series Cricket, taking 7 for 26 against the World XI, including the scalps of Barry Richards, Asif Iqbal and Tony Greig. With a canny eye for business Watson was involved in the design of the Sydney Olympic venue and two of his own homes. He died aged 75 in 2020 in his hometown of Burradoo in the New South Wales Highlands.

Dennis Lillee is generally regarded as Australia's greatest fast bowler. His story is also one of the greatest recoveries from a severe injury in modern-day sports. When his 1973 tour of the West Indies was cut short after a crippling back injury it looked like Lillee's cricket career was over. His sense of discipline and working with sports scientist Dr Frank Pyke enabled an incredible comeback.

Lillee combined with Jeff Thomson to destroy the England batting line-up in 1974/75. In that series, he took 25, followed by 27 wickets in the series against the West Indies the following summer, before capturing a match-winning 11-wicket haul in Australia's 45-run win in the 1977 Centenary Test. In 1981/82 at the MCG Lillee overtook Lance Gibbs' Test wicket record as Australia recorded a rare win against the rampaging West Indies.

He played a key role in the instigation and success of World Series Cricket before retiring in 1984 with 355 Test wickets. Lillee's dramatic appeal and trademark wiping sweat from his brow had been a reminder of Australia's success for more than a decade. Dennis Lillee was President of the WACA for ten years and was elevated to Legend of Sports Hall of Fame status in 2021 after spending much of his retirement mentoring fast bowlers at the MRF Pace Foundation in India (which he set up to establish elite pace bowlers). He worked for the Australian Cricket Board, running a fast bowlers coaching program nationally, and the Australian Cricket Academy, which included Brett Lee, Glenn McGrath, Stuart Clarke and Mitchell Johnson. He now occasionally helps promising young fast bowlers in Australia, gratis.

Bruce Francis joined the International Wanderers for a three-match tour of Rhodesia when the 1972 tour ended. A year later, after another county season with Essex, he appeared for Derrick Robins Eleven in South Africa against a full-strength national line-up. Wanting to stay longer to play provincial cricket and explore the country (he'd majored in African politics during his Economics degree), Francis was told by Australian Board of Control secretary Alan Barnes he'd have to retire from first-class cricket. Francis scored 194 in 223 minutes against Western Province, including a century in a session; teammate John Gleeson described the knock as 'one of the most savage I have ever witnessed'; Keith Stackpole believed 'the cricketing world never got to see the best of Bruce Francis'.

When Francis returned to Australia, he played for Waverley for one more season before retiring at the age of 26. When asked about his 1972 tour, he replied modestly, 'I wasn't very good and shouldn't have been selected in the Australian team' (although he since argued in the journal *Between Wickets* he deserved his place more than Lawry).

Fans growing up in the 1970s would likely remember celebrity cricket matches at the start of each season at Drummoyne Oval in Sydney. Francis helped arrange these, working with Spastic Centre of New South Wales CEO Charlie Price (who had played for the Australian Services side in England at the end of the Second World War). The first match in October 1972 attracted more than 20,000 spectators. By this time, Francis' experience playing for Essex nurtured a friendship with Tony Greig, with Francis managing his accounts between 1975 and 1980. In 1976 Francis met Kerry Packer to talk about what would become World Series Cricket. Francis even coached the young James Packer after his father put down a pitch and nets on vacant land at his Bellevue Hill home, and he later gave his baggy green to James Packer. Francis also organised rebel tours to South Africa and stood for parliament as a member of the Liberal Party. When Cricket Australia awarded all the living Australian players with a miniature baggy green cap and a Test number, Francis felt too embarrassed to attend the function.

The 1972 tour was the last for Brian Taber; he bowed out of first-class cricket at the end of the 1973/74 season. He later became a coach and New South Wales Chairman of Selectors (and selector for a total of 23 seasons) as well as the National Director of Cricket Coaching. He twice toured England, South Africa and India, playing 16 Test matches, taking 56 catches and four stumpings. Taber was made a Life Member of Cricket NSW in 1979 and inducted into the Hall of Fame in 2021. He died on 21 July 2023, aged 83.

Ian Chappell had much to be proud of following the 1972 Ashes. With the promise of attacking cricket, his side had helped attract 383,345 spectators who paid £261,283 – at the time, the highest gate for a Test series. While Australia proved they could match England on the field, the tension the Australian captain experienced with Don Bradman would only grow. Ian Chappell led Australia to a triumphant 4–1 series win against England at home before leading Australia's 1975 tour of England and finishing the series with 192 in the Fourth Test at The Oval. Ian Chappell was the key instigator behind attracting player support for Kerry Packer's World Series Cricket and captained the Australian side. Somewhat reluctantly, he returned to play Test cricket for a final season in 1979/80 before retiring and taking up a commentating role with Channel Nine. Much like Richie Benaud, he became part of the sporting landscape for several decades before joining the ABC in radio commentary. He wrote 18 books about the game and became a wise voice regarding Indigenous affairs and asylum seekers. For Ian Chappell, 1972 represented a significant moment in the rise of Australian cricket throughout the decade.

Epilogue

Australia's successes on the 1972 tour played an obvious role in the rise to dominance of Australian cricket. There's little doubt they enhanced Ian Chappell's status as captain. So much so that many of the former players interviewed for this book commented on how Ian Chappell, having led them while playing for Australia in 1972, became a leader for life.

Chappell's leadership enabled the flowering of Dennis Lillee, Rod Marsh and Greg Chappell's talent, stamping them as world-class players. While an adequate opening partnership had yet to be discovered, Australia's top order had transitioned from being brittle to one that was no longer cowered by opposition pace attacks. The late blooming of Ian Redpath later helped solve the opening batting limitations.

Ross Edwards emerged as a solid middle-order batsman for Australia, and Ashley Mallett arrived as an off spinner of class (despite his greatest success being against India, taking 28 wickets in 1969/70). Keith Stackpole's aggressive opening role complemented Ian Chappell's attacking approach.

Australia's continued success under Chappell had enormous ramifications for the relationship between administrators and players for decades as frustration with the pay and conditions grew. A revolution that didn't surprise Chappell's 1972 counterpart Ray Illingworth, who later recalled,

> We were getting paid peanuts. After ten years of Test cricket, you should have been able to get out of the game and not have financial worries. There were large crowds and a lot of money in the game, and not much was going to the players. Players were retiring from Test cricket and not able to get a job. There was a restlessness in the game, which was wide open for taking.

It is hard to imagine a cricket world without the intervention of Kerry Packer and World Series Cricket. Had Ian Chappell failed in 1972, the game's revolution would surely have been slowed. Could Kerry Packer have found a better Australian cricket ally than Ian Chappell? It's hard to imagine one.

Chappell believed he might have been finished as a player and captain had he not performed on the 1972 tour. In a possible alternative history, if you take Ian Chappell out of Test cricket as early as 1972, it removes the key agitator for improvement for players and a significant symbol of player power. Perhaps given increasing player frustration, as Greg Chappell put it, 'a cricket revolution was always going to happen'. But it wouldn't have occurred at the pace or manner it did. Without the sense of professionalism that was imbued in the West Indian players by Kerry Packer and Clive Lloyd, leading to the West Indies two-decade international dominance, the world's cricketing landscape may have looked quite different.

Tour Statistics compiled by Lawrie Colliver

1972 ASHES

AUSTRALIA — BATTING	M	Inns	NO	Runs	HS		Avg	SR	100	50
KR Stackpole	5	10	1	485	114		53.88	51.10	1	5
GS Chappell	5	10	1	437	131		48.55	43.74	2	1
R Edwards	4	7	1	291	170*		48.50	44.90	1	1
AP Sheahan	2	4	2	90	44*		45.00	29.31	0	0
RW Marsh	5	9	2	242	91		34.57	63.35	0	2
IM Chappell	5	10	0	334	118		33.40	35.60	1	2
DJ Colley	3	4	0	84	54		21.00	52.50	0	1
RJ Inverarity	3	5	1	61	28		15.25	26.06	0	0
JW Gleeson	3	4	1	37	30		12.33	28.68	0	0
AA Mallett	2	3	0	34	20		11.33	23.28	0	0
BC Francis	3	5	0	52	27		10.40	37.95	0	0
KD Walters	4	7	0	54	20		7.71	29.83	0	0
GD Watson	2	4	0	21	13		5.25	48.83	0	0
RAL Massie	4	5	0	22	18		4.40	34.92	0	0
DK Lillee	5	7	4	10	7		3.33	16.12	0	0

AUSTRALIA — BOWLING	M	Balls	Mdns	Runs	Wkts	Avg	RPO	BB	5I	10M
DK Lillee	5	1499	83	548	31	17.67	2.19	6-66	3	1
RAL Massie	4	1195	58	409	23	17.78	2.05	8-53	2	1
RJ Inverarity	3	366	26	90	4	22.50	1.47	3-26	0	0
AA Mallett	2	618	32	269	10	26.90	2.61	5-114	1	0
IM Chappell	5	90	7	27	1	27.00	1.80	1-26	0	0
GD Watson	2	240	14	92	3	30.66	2.30	1-23	0	0
DJ Colley	3	729	20	312	6	52.00	2.56	3-83	0	0
JW Gleeson	3	460	28	157	3	52.33	2.04	2-45	0	0
GS Chappell	5	338	17	125	2	62.50	2.21	1-28	0	0
KR Stackpole	5	102	7	35	0		2.05		0	0
KD Walters	4	30	1	7	0		1.40		0	0

Fielding: RW Marsh 23 (21 ct/2 st), GS Chappell 8, IM Chappell 6, KR Stackpole 4, GD Watson, DL Colley, BC Francis, RJ Inverarity, R Edwards, KD Walters 1 each

ENGLAND — BATTING	M	Inns	NO	Runs	HS	Avg	SR	100	50
B Wood	1	2	0	116	90	58.00	39.05	0	1
AW Greig	5	9	1	288	62	36.00	40.05	0	3
R Illingworth	5	8	2	194	57	32.33	32.27	0	1
JH Hampshire	1	2	0	62	42	31.00	52.54	0	0
BL D'Oliveira	5	9	1	233	50*	29.12	41.83	0	1
APE Knott	5	8	0	229	92	28.62	51.92	0	2
BW Luckhurst	4	8	1	168	96	24.00	32.43	0	1
PH Parfitt	3	6	1	117	51	23.40	29.03	0	1
MJK Smith	3	6	0	140	34	23.33	30.97	0	0

ENGLAND — BATTING	M	Inns	NO	Runs	HS	Avg	SR	100	50
JSE Price	1	2	1	23	19	23.00	60.52	0	0
JH Edrich	5	10	0	218	49	21.80	30.57	0	0
G Boycott	2	4	0	72	47	18.00	43.37	0	0
JA Snow	5	8	0	111	48	13.87	37.62	0	0
N Gifford	3	5	1	50	16*	12.50	28.73	0	0
GG Arnold	3	5	2	28	22	9.33	21.37	0	0
P Lever	1	1	0	9	9	9.00	20.00	0	0
DL Underwood	2	3	2	8	5	8.00	18.60	0	0
KWR Fletcher	1	1	0	5	5	5.00	23.80	0	0

ENGLAND — BOWLING	M	Balls	Mdns	Runs	Wkts	Avg	RPO	BB	5I	10M
DL Underwood	2	750	49	266	16	16.62	2.12	6-45	1	1
GG Arnold	3	665	25	279	13	21.46	2.51	4-62	0	0
JA Snow	5	1235	46	555	24	23.12	2.69	5-57	2	0
R Illingworth	5	528	28	197	7	28.14	2.23	2-32	0	0
BL D'Oliveira	5	498	23	176	5	35.20	2.12	1-13	0	0
JSE Price	1	199	5	115	3	38.33	3.46	2-87	0	0
AW Greig	5	975	44	398	10	39.80	2.44	4-53	0	0
N Gifford	3	204	6	116	1	116.00	3.41	1-18	0	0
P Lever	1	270	11	137	1	137.00	3.04	1-61	0	0
PH Parfitt	3	12	0	10	0		5.00		0	0
BW Luckhurst	4	5	0	5	0		6.00		0	0

Fielding: APE Knott 17 (at ct), AW Greig 8, R Illingworth 6, PH Parfitt 5, MJK Smith 4, BW Luckhurst 3, BL D'Oliveria 3, N Gifford 2, JA Snow 2, JH Hampshire 1, JH Edrich 1

AUSTRALIA - FIRST CLASS TOUR AVERAGES

BATTING	M	Inns	NO	Runs	HS	Avg	100	50
GS Chappell	18	28	10	1260	181	70.00	4	3
KR Stackpole	21	35	5	1309	154*	43.63	3	7
AP Sheahan	17	26	7	788	135*	41.47	1	4
KD Walters	19	29	5	935	154	38.95	3	0
GD Watson	18	27	2	915	176	36.60	2	4
RW Marsh	17	24	5	664	91	34.94	0	5
R Edwards	18	26	3	747	170*	32.47	1	3
IM Chappell	20	34	2	1017	118	31.78	2	6
BC Francis	18	27	1	772	210	29.69	2	4
RJ Inverarity	21	30	9	553	100*	26.33	1	1
JR Hammond	13	6	3	78	36*	26.00	0	0
HB Taber	12	11	3	180	54	22.50	0	1
DJ Colley	16	16	3	268	58*	20.61	0	2
AA Mallett	15	13	3	146	29	14.60	0	0
JW Gleeson	17	12	4	88	30	11.00	0	0
DK Lillee	14	13	7	30	11*	5.00	0	0
RAL Massie	12	10	1	45	18	5.00	0	0

BOWLING — MOST WICKETS	M	Balls	Mdns	Runs	Wkts	Avg	BB	5I	10M
DK Lillee	14	2741	119	1197	53	22.58	6-66	3	1
RAL Massie	12	2290	115	851	50	17.02	8-53	4	2
JW Gleeson	17	2129	106	1014	44	23.04	6-21	2	0
AA Mallett	15	2574	124	1165	41	28.41	5-59	3	0
RJ Inverarity	21	2123	101	983	37	26.56	5-67	1	0

BOWLING — MOST WICKETS	M	Balls	Mdns	Runs	Wkts	Avg	BB	5I	10M
DJ Colley	16	2080	73	946	33	28.66	5-27	2	0
JR Hammond	13	1668	59	809	26	31.11	6-15	2	0
GD Watson	18	1464	64	621	25	24.84	5-36	1	0
GS Chappell	18	1238	49	488	19	25.68	7-58	1	0
IM Chappell	20	263	14	106	10	10.60	3-1	0	0
KD Walters	19	213	6	117	2	58.50	1-10	0	0
KR Stackpole	21	378	20	164	2	82.00	1-12	0	0
BC Francis	18	17	0	15	1	15.00	1-10	0	0
AP Sheahan	17	24	0	19	1	19.00	1-19	0	0
R Edwards	18	18	0	15	0		-	0	0

Fielding: RW Marsh 45 (38 ct/7st), HB Taber 27 (22 ct/ 5 st), GS Chappell 25, IM Chappell 20, KR Stackpole 15, RJ Inverarity 13, R Edwards 9, GD Watson 7, KD Walters 7, AP Sheahan 6, AA Mallett 5, DJ Colley 5, BC Francis 5, JR Hammond 4, DK Lillee 3, JW Gleeson 3

Test Scores

1st Test Old Trafford, June 8–13, 1972. England won by 89 runs

England 249 (JH Edrich 49, AW Greig 57; DJ Colley 3–83) and 234 (G Boycott 47, AW Greig 62: DK Lillee 6–66) defeated **Australia** 142 (KR Stackpole 53: JA Snow 4–41, GG Arnold 4–62) and 252 (KR Stackpole 67, RW Marsh 91; JA Snow 4–87, AW Greig 4–53)

2nd Test Lord's, June 22–26, 1972. Australia won by eight wickets

England 272 (AW Greig 54, APE Knott 43; RAL Massie 8–84) and 116 (RAL Massie 8–53) lost to **Australia** 308 (IM Chappell 56, GS Chappell 131, RW Marsh 50; JA Snow 5–57) and 2–81 (KR Stackpole 57*)

3rd Test Trent Bridge, July 13–18, 1972. Match drawn

Australia 315 (KR Stackpole 114, RW Marsh 41, DJ Colley 54; JA Snow 5–92) and 4–324 dec (R Edwards 170*, IM Chappell 50, GS Chappell 72: JA Snow 3–94) drew with **England** 189 (DK Lillee 4–35, RAL Massie 4–43) and 4–290 (BW Luckhurst 96, PH Parfitt 46, BL D'Oliveria 50*)

4th Test Headingley, July 27–29, 1972. England won by nine wickets

Australia 146 (KR Stackpole 52; DL Underwood 4–37) and 136 (AP Sheahan 41*; DL Underwood 6–45) lost to **England** 263 (JH Edrich 45, R Illingworth 57, JA Snow 48: AA Mallett 5–114, RJ Inverarity 3–26) and 1–21

5th Test The Oval, August 10–16, 1972. Australia won by five wickets

England 284 (PH Parfitt 51, JH Hampshire 42, APE Knott 92; DK Lillee 5–58, AA Mallett 3–80) and 356 (B Wood 90, BL D'Oliveria 43, APE Knott 63; DK Lillee 5–123) lost to **Australia** 399 (IM Chappell 118, GS Chappell 113, R Edwards 79; GG Arnold 3–87; DL Underwood 4–90) and 5–242 (KR Stackpole 79, AP Sheahan 44*, RW Marsh 43*)

Acknowledgements

As with any book, there are many helpers. First, thank you to the former players and press who took the time to speak with me, especially Ian Chappell, who opened several doors and kindly wrote a foreword to this book, as did Dennis Lillee. Ross Edwards was my first point of call. His recollections, scrapbooks and diary were invaluable resources. Ross was always enthusiastic, supportive and kind. Bruce Francis spoke to me and sent me his father's biography, *Cass Francis: An Autobiography, A Life Fulfilled*, which was a great help. Lawrie Colliver happily provided numerous DVDs of Australian cricket during this period as well as the statistical appendage to this book.

Bernard Whimpress' timely advice was a godsend. Michael Sexton, Richard Whitehead and Ken Piesse were a great help in alerting me to and, in some cases, sending me contemporary and retrospective accounts of players and moments during the tour. Mark Clisby, Graham Lewis, Nick Moschetta, Ralph Nicholls, Gary and Greg Slack, Paul Twiss, and Nick White provided terrific support over the six years it took to write this book. Rob Bath, Jonathan Northall and Dan Lonergan proved great readers. Julia Beaven's editorial skills and Michael Bollen's calm guidance have been essential factors in making this book what it is.

Bibliography

Interviews

Ian Brayshaw, Daphne Benaud, Ian Chappell, David Colley, Mike Coward, Ross Edwards, Patrick Eagar, Bruce Francis, Jeff Hammond, John Inverarity, Dennis Lillee, Ashley Mallett, Bob Massie, Paul Sheahan, Keith Stackpole, Doug Walters, Graeme Watson, and Ashley Woodcock.

Newspapers, magazines and annuals

ABC Cricket Book 1972, *Advertiser*, *Australian Cricket*, *News*, *Cricketer* (Australia), *John Player Cricket Yearbook 1973*, *The Cricketer* (UK), *Daily Post*, *Daily Telegraph*, *Sun* (UK), *Sunday Mail*, *The Australian*, *World of Cricket*, *Sunday Times* (Perth), *West Australian*, *Wisden Cricketers' Almanack 1970, 1971, 1972, 1973*.

Books

Arlott, John. *The Ashes 1972*, Pelham Books, Great Britain, 1972.

Benaud, John. *Matters of Choice: A Test Selector's Story*, Swan Publishing Pty Ltd, Dalkeith, WA, 1997.

Brayshaw, Ian. *Caught Marsh bowled Lillee: The legend lives on*, ABC Books, Sydney, 2001.

Cannane, Steve. *First Tests: Great Australian Cricketers and the Backyards That Made Them*, ABC Books, 2009.

Chappell, Ian. *Tigers Among the Lions*, Lynton Publications Pty Ltd, South Australia, 1972.

Crook, Frank. *Talking Cricket with Frank Crook*, ABC Enterprises, Sydney, 1989.

Cardwell, Ronald and Jenkins, David. *It's Not About Me: The Brian Taber Story*, The Cricket Publishing Company, West Pennant Hills, 2014.

Coward, Mike. *The Chappell Years: Cricket in the 1970s*, ABC Books, Sydney, 2002.

Egan, Jack. *Extra Cover: Twenty-six interviews with players and people behind the scenes in Australian cricket*, Pan Books, Sydney, 1989.

Haigh, Gideon. *The Summer Game*, Text Publishing Company, Melbourne, 1997.

Haigh, Gideon and Frith, David. *Inside Story: Unlocking Australian Cricket Archives*, News Custom Publishing, Melbourne, 2007.

Illingworth, Ray. *Spinner's Wicket*, Stanley Paul, UK, 1969.

Knott, Alan. *It's Knott Cricket: The autobiography of Alan Knott*, MacMillan, London, 1985.

Lillee, Dennis. *My Life in Cricket*, Methuen Australia Pty Ltd, Hawthorn,1982.

Mallett, Ashley. *Great Australian Test Cricket Stories*, ABC Books, Sydney, 2017.

Mallett, Ashley with Ian Chappell. *Chappelli Speaks Out*, Allen & Unwin, Sydney, 2005.

Mallett, Ashley. *One of a Kind: The Doug Walters Story*, Allen & Unwin, NSW, 2008.

Mallett, Ashley. *Rowdy*, Lynton Publications Pty Ltd, Blackwood, South Australia, 1973.

Marsh, Rod. *You'll Keep*, Hutchinson, Victoria, 1975.

Redpath, Ian and Phillipson, Neill. *Always Ready*, Garry Sparke & Associates, Toorak, Victoria, 1976.

Sexton, Michael. *Chappell's Last Stand*, Affirm Press, Melbourne, 2017.

Snow, John. *Cricket Rebel*, Hamlyn, United Kingdom, 1976.

Sandbrook, Dominic. *State of Emergency, The Way We Were: Britain, 1970–1974*, Penguin Books UK, 2011.

Snow, John. *Cricket Rebel: An autobiography*, Hamlyn Publishing Group Limited, London, 1976.

Stackpole, Keith with Alan Trengrove. *Not Just for Openers*, Stockwell Press, Victoria, 1974.

Webster, Ray. *First Class Cricket in Australia Vol. 2 1945/46 to 1976/77*, self-published, Victoria, 1997.

Whimpress, Bernard. *On Our Selection: An Alternative History of Australian Cricket*, self-pub., South Australia, 2011.

Whitington, R.S. *Captains Outrageous: Cricket in the Seventies*, Hutchinson Group Pty Ltd, London, 1972.

Wilshire, Jeremy. *Test of Character: Confessions of Cricket Legends*, Echo Publishing, Victoria, 2016.

www.ingramcontent.com/pod-product-compliance
Ingram Content Group Australia Pty Ltd
76 Discovery Rd, Dandenong South VIC 3175, AU
AUHW021054180725
414038AU00002B/2

9 781923 042841